Discover

Guernsey
Alderney, Sark

Cover picture: early morning sunshine touches the waterfront at St Peter Port.

Discover

Guernsey

Alderney, Sark

Terry Palmer

HERITAGE
HOUSE

Discover Guernsey, Alderney, Sark
First published March 1994
ISBN 1.85215.0386
Typesetting extrapolated in 8.5 on 9.5 Rockwell on Linotron
300 by Anglia Photoset, St Botolph St, Colchester, from in-
house computer setting.
Printed by Colorcraft Ltd, Hong Kong.
Published by Heritage House (Publishers) Ltd, King's Rd,
Clacton-on-Sea, CO15 1BG.

   Titles in the 'Discover' series, in print or in preparation, include:
Discover Cyprus and North Cyprus
Discover The Dominican Republic
Discover Florida
Discover The Gambia
Discover Guernsey, Alderney, Sark
Discover Gibraltar
Discover The Grand Canyon State
Discover Hungary
Discover Jersey
Discover Malta
Discover Poland
Discover Sardinia
Discover Tunisia
Discover Seychelles
...and several of the English regions.

CONTENTS

1: Why Guernsey? 7
2: Tomato Salad 9
3: The Constitution 19
4: Sarnia's Story 29
5: Les Iles Normandes 33
6: Hitler's Fortress Isles 43
7: Isles of Legend 49
8: Guernsey 54
9: Alderney 83
10: Sark 93
11: Herm and Jethou 101
12: When the Sun Goes Down 107

MAPS

Alderney 86
The Bailiwick of Guernsey 6
The Channel Islands 21
Guernsey 66-67
Herm 104
Saint Peter Port . . . . · · 53
Sark 97

Terry Palmer (above) published his first guide book to the Channel Islands in 1977, and has been back many times since – coming by air, by car ferry, and even flying with the Royal Mail from Southend-on-Sea when he was press officer with the Post Office.

His connections with Guernsey run deeper, as a cousin from Nottingham moved his family to St Martin in the 1970s and became involved in the airport, air freight and container transport business.

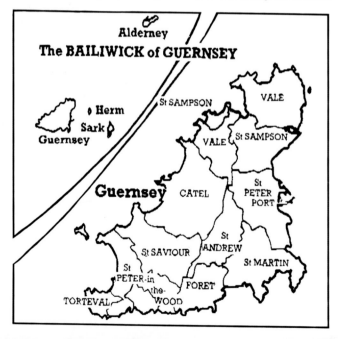

1: WHY GUERNSEY?

So different, yet so similar

GUERNSEY AND ITS SISTER-ISLANDS were never conquered by Britain. In fact, the reverse is true: the Channel Islands, as part of Normandy, conquered England in 1066. Since around 933 when Rollo added the islands to the Dukedom of Normandy, the inhabitants have been answerable only to the duke and his successors – with the present successor being the British Sovereign.

How big? Guernsey is the second-largest of the Channel Islands, a granite outcrop covering 15,654 acres (24.45sq miles, 63.34sq km), with a population of 55,400 in 1986, giving a density of 2,266 people per square mile (875p sq km); Jersey has 28,717 acres (44.87sq miles, 116.18sq km); Alderney has 1,962 acres (3.06sq miles, 7.94sq km); Sark with Brechou claims 1,348 acres (2.1sq miles, 5.44sq km) including the 239ac (95ha) of Little Sark; and Herm has just 320 acres (0.5sq mile exact, 1.3sq km); while Jethou, not open to visitors, is 44 acres small (18ha). Add Jersey's 28,717 acres (44.8sq miles, 116.2sq km) and you have a land mass of 75 square miles (147sq km) that is one third the size of the Isle of Man but with twice as many people, and nearly half the size of the Isle of Wight. On a world scale, the Channel Islands would fit into Andorra twice, and the American state of Rhode Island 16 times.

Tomatoes. For generations Guernsey grew vegetables for the British market, eventually concentrating on glasshouse tomatoes and flowers; if you flew over the island in the late 1970s you would be dazzled by the sun reflecting off hundreds of acres of glass which produced 9,000,000 trays of tomatoes each year. An overflight in the 1990s would show far less dazzle, and many of the remaining glasshouses about to collapse, like the market for their produce. In 1992 just 1,000,000 trays went to Britain and at the end of that season more growers left the business, which can no longer compete with

Dutch exports. Some growers tried kiwi fruit, but found that market even more fickle; a few have turned their greenhouses into tourist attractions, but most have quietly abandoned them.

Tourism and finance. So Guernsey, like Jersey, has gone into the tourist and financial services industries. Tourism has much to offer: the unique history of the Channel Islands which has resulted in two self-governing bailiwicks, with Guernsey in particular having the attraction of its lesser islands – cosy Sark, where a benign feudalism still survives; windswept Alderney, with more fortresses per inhabitant than anywhere else in Europe; and tiny Herm.

The absence of party politics in the islands has resulted in stable governments in each of the bailiwicks, which in turn has attracted many banks and financiers. The low tax levels have also helped, but these have made the islands so attractive to 'outsiders' that Guernsey and Jersey have had to impose strict residence qualifications and develop a two-tier housing market.

Houses. In both islands there is a 'local' and an 'open' list of properties, with outsiders obliged to buy only in the open list, where prices are vastly higher. Strangely, Alderney and Sark don't have this problem: you can buy a house in Alderney and move straight in, and if you buy one of the original 40 settlements on Sark, where there is no Income Tax at all, you automatically find yourself a member of the island's parliament, the Chief Pleas.

Stamps and banknotes. Since 1969 the bailiwicks have run their own postal services, giving rise to commemorative stamps for Sark and Alderney, although it meant the end of the collectable Herm stamp. Guernsey also issues its own currency, including the one-pound note, but British and Jersey money is perfectly acceptable.

The islands have other attractions: they are very French while still being staunchly British, and English-speaking; they were the only parts of the British Empire to fall into Nazi hands during World War Two; and each is so very different in its own way from Britain and from each other, without losing its Britishness.

Taxes. If you want further incentives, then consider that car hire in Guernsey is among the cheapest in the world; petrol is almost half the British cost; and as the islands are not full members of the European Community none has Value Added Tax. Indeed, Sark has its own duty-free allowance for people going to Guernsey or Jersey.

French islands. But beware: some of the Channel Islands are French. The Iles Chausey returned to French rule with the Peace of Aix-la-Chapelle in 1668, and when the French claimed the Roches Douvres reef in 1869, Britain didn't contest it. The last territorial problem was settled in 1953 when the International Court at The Hague decided that the Minquiers and the Ecréhous reefs were British.

2: TOMATO SALAD

Facts and figures

GUERNSEY HAS ITS OWN GOVERNMENT, taxation system, and motoring laws. Visitors find the first two to be matters of interest, but if you're going to drive in Guernsey you should know the basic laws of motoring.

MOTORING

Left. Drive on the left, as in Britain. You can take your car to Guernsey, and to Alderney via France, and you can hire cars in both islands. There is no point in taking your car to Herm, and cars are not allowed at all on Sark where the only mechanised transport comes from tractors.

Number plates. Guernsey registrations are all figures; on Alderney the figures are prefixed by AY; licence plates are not needed on Herm or Sark. As a matter of interest, AY cars that don't leave the island, needn't have an annual roadworthiness test. Jersey plates carry the J prefix, and the G prefix belongs far away in Gibraltar.

Speed limits. The maximum speed limit in Guernsey is 35mph (56kph), with limits in built-up areas usually 25mph (40kph) but dropping much lower in certain parts.

Seat belts. Seat belt regulations apply as in Britain and most other countries.

Parking. Parking is difficult everywhere. In St Peter Port you'll need a **parking disc** available for 60p at the tourist office on the quay, at the police station, or free with your hire car. Set it to show the time you parked, and move on before the end of your permitted stay, shown by signs; it ranges from 10 hours down to 15 minutes. There are no parking fees, but the fine is £10 if you overstay your welcome.

Parking is difficult in rural areas because Guernsey has a network of lanes, most of them narrow and twisting, screened by hedges or walls, and few with a pavement (sidewalk). Don't park where the road is edged with a single yellow line.

Map. You *will* need a good map of the island, but even so you should reckon on getting lost at least once a day. Fortunately, you'll seldom be more than a mile off course.

"I may be just a cow, but I helped build the island's prosperity."

There are few road signs, although the States is planning to add some. Get a map which names all the roads, and use this as an extra navigational aid.

Petrol. Petrol is available throughout the island, with most service stations open into the evening, but **all are closed on Sundays.** Prices are approximate: unleaded, 30p litre (£1.35 gallon); 4-star 31p litre (£1.36 gallon); diesel 24p litre (£1.10 gallon). Fuel is marginally cheaper in Jersey.

Road signs. A yellow line across your road indicates a junction with a priority road; a yellow arrow further back would have given you warning of the junction.

Several junctions have FILTER IN TURN painted on their approach roads; it's self-explanatory and means nobody has priority.

Caravans. Caravans and motorised caravans are not allowed on any of the islands – the reasons are obvious when you see the width of the roads. If you have a choice between a Jaguar and a Mini, leave the Jag at home.

Alderney. Alderney is much easier for motorists, as the country-side is open and you can often see half the length of the island. Parking in the centre of St Anne is difficult.

Car hire agencies. Car hire is easy to arrange, but if you're doing it independently, give as much notice as possible, and check any age limits that may apply. This list is from the Guernsey and Alderney tourist boards:

Avis Rent-a-Car, Guernsey Airport, ✆35266
Al Car Hire, North Esplanade, St Peter Port, ✆712228
Baubigny Car Hire, Baubigny, St Sampson's, ✆45855
Budget Rent-a-Car, Airport, ✆64146
Easy Rent, Les Banques, St Peter Port ✆710257
Economy Cars, Rue du Pré, St Peter Port ✆726926
Falles Hire Cars, Airport Rd, Forest, ✆36902
Godfrey Davis Eurocar, Airport, ✆37638
Harlequin Hire Cars, PO Box 258, La Route de Roulias, Forest, ✆39511
Hertz Rent-a-Car, Airport, ✆65860
Kingslea Car Hire, Strawberry Farm, Le Gron, St Saviour's ✆65679
Rent-a-Renault, The Grange, St Peter Port ✆726846
Sarnia Hire Cars, Stanley Rd, St Peter Port ✆723933
ALDERNEY:
Alderney Taxis & Hire Cars, ✆822611, 822992
Grand Self-drive, Mount Hale House, Arsenal, ✆822848.

CYCLE HIRE

Guernsey is relatively easy for the cyclist, the main problem being other traffic on the narrow lanes, but roads down to the bays on the south coast are very steep. Sark is easier, and cycling is the most convenient way of seeing the island. Gradients are reasonable, but all roads have grit surfaces. Cycling is easiest of all on Alderney's tarmac roads, but there are a few steep hills.

Island Cycle Hire, North Plantation, St Peter Port ✆711807
Millard & Co, Victoria Rd, St Peter Port ✆720777
Moullins Cycle Shop, St George's Esplanade, St Peter Port ✆721581
Perrio's, Chescot, Route Carré, L'Islet, St Sampson's, ✆45217
Cycle & Unipart Shop, The Bridge, St Sampson's ✆49311
West Coast Cycles, Les Tamaris, Portinfer Lane, Vale, ✆53654
Wheel House Cycle Hire, Lindale, Rue Maze, St Martin's, ✆36815
ALDERNEY:
J.B. Cycle Hire, Val Garages, ✆822294, 822762
Top Gear Cycle Hire, Melford House, Le Banquage, ✆822000
Pedal Power, Les Roquettes, ✆822286
SARK:
In high season reserve a cycle or carriage ride when you book your ferry passage with the Isle of Sark Shipping Co. Off-season, you can save the small booking fee and take your chance with the cycle agencies behind the Bel Air Tavern or on The Avenue.

MOPEDS

You will need your driving licence to hire a moped, and it's a good idea to bring your helmet.

GUERNSEY: Millard, Victoria Rd, St Peter Port, ✆720777
ALDERNEY: Alderney Moped Hire, Ollivier St, ✆823710.

BUSES

Guernseybus, formerly the Guernsey Railway Company, runs the island's bus service, radiating from St Peter Port to almost everywhere on the island. Monday to Saturday in high summer there are up to 10 services on each route, which usually operate on a small loop, coming back to the starting place in 'town.' Here's a summary of destinations:

B: Jerbourg, Icart, and reverse.

C1: Airport, Torteval, Pleinmont, Fort Grey, Airport.

C2: same route, reverse direction.

D: Little Chapel, L'Erée, Le Gron, Little Chapel.

E: Bailiff's Cross, King's Mills, Perelle, Vazon, King's Mills.

F: Saumarez Park, Cobo Bay, Vazon Bay, and return; also in reverse order.

G: Saumarez Park, Cobo Bay, Beau Séjour; and reverse.

H1: Camp du Roi, L'Islet, Guernsey Candles.

H2: similar to H1.

J1: up to 15 services daily to St. Sampson's, L'Ancresse, Bordeaux.

J2: J1 in reverse.

K: up to 6 services daily on a sightseeing coastal route, possibly in a former London double-deck bus. St Sampson's, Bordeaux, L'Ancresse, Grand Havre, Grandes Rocques, L'Erée, Pleinmont, and return.

L1: L'Islet and return.

L2: Vale, L'Ancresse, Pembroke, and return.

Tourist Tripper: Introduced in 1992 and visiting the Underground Hospital, Little Chapel, Petit Bot Bay, Airport, Les Grands Moulins and Saumarez Park.

Tours. In addition there are set bus tours, mostly leaving at 1415 on selected days. Destinations are the Butterfly Farm, Tomato Centre, Little Chapel, and Guernsey Pottery, with a Morning Coast Tour leaving at 1030.

Tram. Island Coachways, one of several coach companies, operates the tram daily from the Clocktower by the town's north beach to the Aquarium, and return. The tram is really a diesel-engined bus with a special body, but it's something different. The fare is 50p each way.

ALDERNEY. Small buses run from Marais Sq in St Anne to Braye, Mannez, Longis Rd, and back to Marais Sq. Several minibus excursions operate: **Alderney Taxis & Hire Cars,** Victoria St, ✆823532; **Alderney Tours,** ✆822260; **Marina Cabs,** ✆823707; and **Riduna Buses,** ✆823359. The latter offers commentaries in English, French, German and Dutch.

ALDERNEY RAILWAY COMPANY

The only surviving railway on the islands operates between Braye Harbour, Alderney, and Mannez Quarry. The route was part of a larger network built to carry stone to the harbour, and its most noteworthy passenger was Queen Victoria. The restored section runs Easter-Sep, Sat, Sun, bank hols; Wed during school hols; 1400 and 1600 from Braye; £1.50 return. Coaches are either ex-London Underground or small open wagons with a simple roof, and the locos are diesel or steam.

SARK HORSE CARRIAGES

Sark's carriages operate during the main season Mon-Sat, according to ferry times. Pick-up point is at the top of Harbour Hill, 300ft (100m) above sea level, and the carriages cover set routes, which do not include Little Sark. The usual fare is £4.

INTER-ISLAND FERRIES

From Britain. British Channel Island Ferries runs the year-round car ferry from Poole to Guernsey and Jersey, but not to France. Reservations: ✆0202.681155. **Condor** has a high-speed car-carrying trimaran service from Weymouth to the two main islands, Mar-Nov. Reservations: ✆0305.761551.

To France. Condor links St Peter Port and St Helier with St Malo in

It's not unusual for visitors to arrive at St Peter's Church, Sark, by horse carriage.

France, Mar-Nov. Reservations in Guernsey: ✆726121. The French **Emeraude Ferries** takes cars year-round from Guernsey via Jersey to St Malo, and passengers by fast catamaran to Carteret, Granville, and Portbail on the Cotentin peninsula. Reservations in Guernsey: ✆711414. *Sea Fox* (see Alderney) takes passengers to Dielette on the Cotentin, either direct or **via Sark.** Days and times are irregular; see the timetable. *Trondenes* sails *from Cherbourg* Wed and Thurs; see Alderney.

To Jersey: Twice-daily (summer), daily (winter) car ferries with BCIF; four sailings daily (Apr-Sep) in Condor trimaran.

To Sark: From **Guernsey,** via the Isle of Sark Shipping Co passenger-only ferries, sailing from White Rock (by the BCIF loading ramp); frequent summer services Mon-Sat, less in winter. The only Sunday sailing is to collect people who have been staying on Sark. From **Jersey** on Emeraud Lines' Trident catamaran, Apr-Sep, Mon-Sat, and on to St Malo. This service does not call at Guernsey.

To Herm: Four companies operate this short route, all from St Peter Port. **Herm Express,** ✆721342; **Herm Seaways,** ✆724677; **Munson Herm Ferry,** 722613; and **Travel Trident,** ✆721379. Passengers only.

To Alderney: *Sea Fox* may operate a Saturday charter service, depending on demand; ✆714022. Otherwise you must fly with Aurigny Air Services.

Alderney to France: *Sea Fox* takes 65 passengers to Goury, near Cherbourg, with two crossings on Tues, Thur, Fri, Sat, but as the boat is based in France there is effectively one chance for a day trip to the continent. Sailing times vary, so ✆010.33.33.04.09.36 (Goury) or ✆823767 (Alderney).

Alderney businessmen were indignant about the price of farm produce that Jerseymen were charging them, so they bought their own ship, *Trondenes,* and began operating her in July 1992 as a car and cargo ferry based in Cherbourg. She sails from there to Alderney on Tues, and to Guernsey Wed and Thur, times depending on tides. Inquiries: Alderney, ✆822818l; Guernsey, ✆713788; Cherbourg, ✆010.33.33.44.25.55.

TIDES

The high tide, surging in from the Atlantic on a front 130 miles (200km) wide between Cornwall and Brittany, meets the Cotentin peninsula and is suddenly funnelled into a gap 60 miles (100km) wide between Poole and Cherbourg. The result is the strongest tidal surge in Europe, exceeding that through the Strait of Gibraltar. The fastest currents of all, reaching 10 knots (16kmh) maximum, are The Swinge north-west of Alderney and The Race on the south-east, plainly visible if you fly into Alderney at the right state of the tide. Elsewhere, vast areas of rock and sand are exposed at low water, particularly

Aurigny is the only airline to use Alderney Airport. Islander aircraft such as this are mostly replaced by Trislanders.

between Guernsey and Herm.

The **maximum tidal range** in St Peter Port, ignoring storm surges, is 32ft (9.75m), and it's worth noting that **spring tides,** the highest, associated with the new and the full moon, come around noon, GMT. Remember: *holiday at full moon, high tide's at noon.*

AIR LINKS

Guernsey has air links with 20 British towns and cities, and 12 on the continent, as well as with Alderney and Jersey.

Aurigny Air Services is the only airline to use Alderney's small airport, flying Britten-Norman Trislander aircraft with seating for 14 passengers. The airline started in 1968 and now calls at Southampton, Bournemouth, Dinard, Cherbourg, Guernsey and Jersey.

Every passenger has a window seat, and the lucky one can watch the pilot's hands on the controls and read the dials – but there's no in-flight service.

DISABLED VISITORS

Disabled visitors are welcome, including those confined to wheelchairs, but there are limits on what can be done and seen.

The **impossible:** travel to Sark and Herm, and on the buses. The **difficult:** visiting Castle Cornet and some backstreets in St Peter Port; flying to Alderney. Most other activities are possible, but contact the Inspector of Hotels, PO Box 23, St Peter Port, ☏726611 (fax 721246) for a list of suitable hotels. Also ask for the leaflet *Access in Guernsey.*

COST OF LIVING

There is no Value Added Tax in the Channel Islands, and all other taxes are lower than in Britain and France – but there is the extra cost of freight for imported goods.

These are sample prices in Guernsey:

Smirnoff Red Label vodka, litre	£10.60
– Blue Label, litre	£12.15
Gilbey's gin, litre	£10.50
Lamb's Navy rum, litre	£10.20
Bacardi rum, litre	£11.75
Bell's Extra Special whisky, 70cl	£8.20
Mouton Cadet blanc, 75cl	£4.50
Bristol Cream sherry, 70cl	£5.30
top brand cigarettes, 200	£13.60 – £14.

These are sample prices on Sark, which has no direct taxation at all:

Bucktrouts vodka, litre	£5.40
– gin, litre	£5.60
Bisquit cognac, 75cl	£9.50
Lamb's Navy rum, 75cl	£9.50

Draw your own conclusions. The duty-free allowance from Sark is 20 cigarettes and 1 litre of spirits, but your full allowance applies if you are leaving the islands within 48 hours.

MONEY and BANKS

The Bailiwick of Guernsey issues its own currency, with notes of £1, £5, £10 and £20; there is no £50 note. Coinage is identical to that in Britain, but minted specially for the bailiwick. **The money is accepted throughout the islands, but nowhere else.** In addition, Alderney issues its own limited-edition £2 coins in gold, silver or cupro-nickel, mainly for collectors, although they are legal tender on the island.

Banking hours. Banks close earlier than in Britain – 0930-1530 – with a few staying open later. You'll find Barclays, Lloyds, Midland and NatWest, and the Royal Bank of Scotland. You may also see up to 40 other banking houses including some from Australia, Bermuda, Belgium, Canada, Italy, Switzerland and the USA, indicating how important the offshore banking business is to the island's economy.

Alderney has Lloyds, Midland and NatWest, open 1000-1200, 1400-1500; and Sark just has the latter two, open the same hours.

Sovereign's head. In 1813 the States of Guernsey asked the Privy Council for permission to have copper coins, minted in Birmingham. The council agreed, provided the Royal Mint had the contract.

The States didn't like being told what to do, so delayed the striking of the coins until 1830, when it used its preferred mint, that of Boulton

Following a disagreement in the early 19th century, no Guernsey banknote carries the sovereign's head. This £1 note was printed by a firm established by Guernseyman Thomas de la Rue.

& Co, in Birmingham. As the States had not followed Privy Council directions, it omitted the sovereign's head from the coins, which it still does to this day. Another strange fact is that French money was legal tender in Guernsey until 1921.

MISCELLANEOUS

Phoning home. The area code for Guernsey, Alderney and Sark is **0481**, which need not be dialled for any numbers within the bailiwick. The code for Jersey is 0534.

To dial a British number, use only the area code and the number; to dial a French number, prefix it with 010.33 (00.33 from April 1995).

Phone boxes give instructions in English, French, and Portuguese, this last for the many migrant workers.

Dress. Topless bathing is acceptable on public beaches, but is not common. Shirts and shoes are required dress in most shops. Come prepared for at least one rainy day.

Electricity. 240v AC, as in Britain. British plugs fit island sockets.

Flag. Guernsey's flag, adopted in 1958, shows the cross of St George with the Papal cross superimposed. Alderney's flag has a motif with a lion *rampant* on St George's cross, while Sark's cross of St George has two Normandy leopards *couchant* in the top left canton.

Licensing hours. Public houses may open between 1000 and 2345 Mon-Sat. Alcohol is on sale on Sunday only in licensed restaurants.

Military service. Channel Islanders have always been exempt from military service outside the islands, unless it be to rescue the sovereign. They may volunteer to join the British forces.

Shopping hours. Normally 0900-1730 Mon-Sat, but some close at 1230 on Thurs in winter.

Public holidays. As in Britain, plus 9 May, Liberation Day, marking the islands' emergence from German occupation. This is not celebrated in Alderney, which was completely evacuated.

Religion. Each of the ten parishes has its own Protestant church, with the entire islands coming in the Diocese of Winchester, although the Catholic churches are part of the Diocese of Portsmouth.

Tourist offices. Guernsey: PO Box 23, White Rock, St Peter Port – it's on Crown Pier – ✆0481.723552, fax ~714951   Open Mon-Sat 0900-2000, Sun 1000-1300, 1800-2000.

Alderney: Victoria St, St Anne, ✆0481.822994 (answerphone).

Sark: at the top of Harbour Hill; most inquiries covered by Guernsey office, ✆0481.832345.

CALENDAR of EVENTS

The Bailiwick's schedule of events changes year by year, but this is an *approximation* of what you may find:

March, early, Guernsey Eisteddfod.

April, late, Festival of Food and Wine.

May, early, Jazz weekend; first Sunday **in Alderney,** Milk-a-Punch Sunday, free punch in the island's pubs, perpetuating a tradition of being allowed to take milk and egg from anyone's livestock and make a punch drink.

June, mid, St Peter Port Carnival.

July, early, Viaer Marchi ('Old Market'); evening of folklore; late, Harbour Carnival; National Trust Costume Display; Folk Festival; Harbour Carnival; in **Sark,** rowing race to Jersey.

August, early, Rocquaine Regatta; late, Battle of Flowers at North Agricultural Show.

September, early, International Powerboat Week; late, Guernsey Festival.

A rooftop view of Castle Cornet with Sark on the skyline.

3: THE CONSTITUTION

And moving in

TO UNDERSTAND HOW THE ISLANDS ARE GOVERNED, it's essential to appreciate some of their history. They were a part of Normandy when its duke, Guillaume, conquered England in 1066 and became King William I as well as Duke of Normandy. But when King John 'Lackland' lost the mainland of Normandy to Philip II of France in 1204, the Channel Islands stayed loyal to the English Crown, which still symbolised the Normandy Dukedom.

In return, John granted them rights and privileges which, even in 1215, made them virtually self-governing, subject only to the Royal assent and enacted through the Privy Council.

In England, the monarchy gradually lost much of its power to Parliament, but the Channel Islanders, like the Manxmen, clung tenaciously to their precious freedom.

Feudalism. As England developed a parliamentary democracy, these little islands on the edge of France stayed in their feudal past. The manors – *fiefs*, pronounced 'fee-effs' – created by the Normans, survived the pressures of change and are now the basis of the islands' governments. Sark is an excellent example as its sole manor has survived intact, and its Lord of the Manor, known as the *Seigneur*, is now the hereditary head of one of Europe's last truly feudal societies: the other is Andorra, ruled jointly by the Bishop of Urgel for Spain, and the Compte de Foix for France – but the compte is now the French President.

Across the islands, those manors which fell into Crown ownership are known as *Fiefs de la Reine* (or *Roy* when the sovereign is a king): Jersey, for example, has such fiefs in all but two of its parishes.

Warden. The first ruler of the islands was a Warden, appointed by the English Crown. Early wardens were called 'Captain,' but as they gradually took on a military role they became 'Governor.' Later governors seldom bothered to take up residence in the islands, preferring to appoint their own Lieutenant-Governor, *lieu-tenant* being French for 'place-holding,' or the man-on-the-spot. Inevitably, the governorship faded out entirely.

Royal Courts. King John established a Royal Court to dispense justice, its chief officer or *Bailiff* (the word means 'official in a court of law' and is similar to the Scots 'bailie') being helped by 12 *jurats*. In Norman French they were probably called *hommes juguers* but, like the modern 'jury,' the name comes from the Latin verb *jurare*, to swear, as on an oath,

The office of Bailiff, taking over from the Sénéschal of Normandy, gradually came to represent the civil authority, his territory being the *bailiwick*. Then, during the Wars of the Roses, beginning in 1455, the administration of the islands was split into two bailiwicks, Guernsey and Jersey – Sark was uninhabited and Alderney was leased privately from the Crown.

Gradually each island developed its own style of government, in Guernsey the Bailiff and his jurats calling upon other islanders to give advice and opinions. By the mid-18th cent a separate body, the States of Deliberation, had developed as the civil government, separate from the Royal Court although the Bailiff and his jurats sat on both.

A century later, the first of the people's deputies were elected into the States; after World War Two the appointed jurats were replaced by *conseillers* elected by the rest of the States, then in 1993 they faced election by the islanders, each candidate having to canvass all 10 parishes.

States of Deliberation. The modern States is made up this way:

Bailiff (or his deputy), appointed by the Crown
12 Conseillers, elected by island-wide vote
33 People's Deputies, elected by parish vote
10 Douzaine representatives, one voted from each parish
2 Representatives from Alderney
Her Majesty's Procurer (attorney-general, appointed)
Her Majesty's Comptroller (solicitor-general, appointed)

To form the States of Guernsey they are joined by the **States of Election:**

12 Jurats (magistrates, appointed until retirement)
10 Rectors (the parish priests)
24 Douzeniers (see below)
2 more Representatives from Alderney

People's Deputies are voted in for a three-year term; in addition each parish elects a dozen people – in Britain this would be the parish council – known, not surprisingly, as the Douzeniers; each year, every parish chooses which one of its Douzeniers is to sit in the States of Election.

The combined body, the States of Guernsey, which still meets in the Royal Court off St James's St, is the government of the bailiwick in all matters except defence and diplomatic representation, which Britain handles. The States is not obliged to accept any law that Westminster may pass, but it usually does so, often with some modification – for example, it is illegal to sell alcohol and petrol in the bailiwick on Sunday, and the laws of bankrupty and inheritance are based on old Norman custom.

Privy Council. The States is not the final arbiter, as all Bills must be submitted to the Privy Council for Royal Assent before they become law.

Connétable. But that's not all. Each parish in Guernsey – and Jersey, too – elects its *Connétables* to collect parish taxes and, when needed, to help the uniformed police constables in law enforcement: if a Guernsey civilian demands to see your driving licence, he may be a connétable.

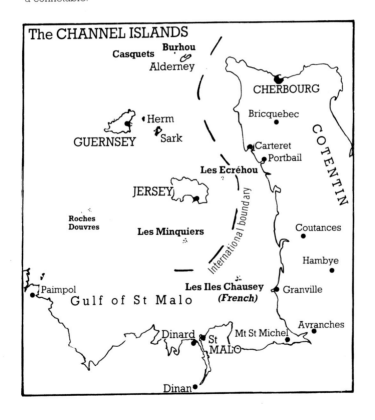

The CHANNEL ISLANDS

ALDERNEY

Alderney adds a minor complication to the story. The first Governor of this isle was appointed in 1660 and the last, one of several to bear the name John le Mesurier, sold his rights-patent to the title in 1825, after which the Lieutenant-Governor of Guernsey held the reins of power. But to complicate the issue, the States of Alderney still ruled the island.

Alderney's total independence ended in 1949 when much of the island government's duties were transferred to the States of Guernsey – hence the representation there – but from that year Alderney emerged with something unique in the islands: an elected President, helped by 12 elected jurats.

SARK

Sark is a major complication to the story: it comes within the Bailiwick of Guernsey but has no representation on the States as it has its own government, the Chief Pleas.

World's smallest country? So here we have an island of 1,348 acres (2.1 square miles, 5.5sq km) with a population in 1984 of just 420 people – and its own government. Based on area, the Vatican City at 109 acres (44ha) must be the world's smallest country, with Monaco second and Gibraltar third, but based on population, Sark could be the world's smallest.

The question is: how do you define a country? Pitcairn had 49 people in 1990 and its own island council, but the Governor lives in New Zealand. Tristan da Cunha has 300 but, like Pitcairn, it is a 'dependent territory' subject to Westminster. Sark is dependent on Guernsey for police, currency and postage – but independent Andorra was equally dependent on France and Spain for years.

Good Queen Bess. St Magliore was probably the first inhabitant of Sark in recorded history, but he died in 587. From the 12th cent, monks from Montebourg on the Cotentin lived here, until Henry V evicted them around 1412. The isle became a haven for pirates until Helier de Carteret, the Seigneur of St Ouen in Jersey decided to recolonise it to keep the French away. He took his letters-patent direct from Queen Elizabeth I and his descendants have owed allegiance direct to the Crown ever since, bypassing Governors and Bailiffs.

Chief Pleas. The government that emerged on Sark, the Chief Pleas, is made up thus:

> The Seigneur, a hereditary title
> 1 Sénéschal, appointed by Seigneur for 3 years
> 12 Deputies, elected for 3 years
> Tenants, as long as they qualify

You needn't speak French to enjoy Guernsey, but it's advisable to know the meaning of these few words.

Every person who owns one of the original 40 homes on Sark is a 'tenant,' using the word in its French meaning of 'holder.' The tenants are therefore the largest group in the Pleas.

The Seigneur can veto any resolution the Pleas makes but, since 1951, the Chief Pleas can resubmit it. Guernsey's Royal Court can also object to proposed laws, which must be approved by the Sovereign and Privy Council.

From 1583 the judge and five jurats were elected by the islanders, but when Charles II demanded that all public officials in his realm belong to the Church of England, Sark was in trouble as its jurats were Presbyterians. The Chief Pleas asked Charles if just *one* Anglican could be appointed, which created the post of Sénéschal, who is both judge and jury.

Today the sénéschal refers all cases to Guernsey if the punishment could exceed a fine of £10 or a prison sentence of 48 hours, and Sark's tiny prison has become a tourist attraction.

The Chief Pleas meets on three Wednesdays in the year: after 15 January, after Easter, and after Michaelmas, with much of its work being delegated to the 20 committees, the oldest and most important being the Douzaine. In addition, the Seigneur appoints a *Prévôt* to collect any fines, a *Greffier* to act as Clerk of the Court, and a *Treasurer* to fill the role of Chancellor of the Exchequer; all duties are part-time and unpaid.

FEUDALISM

Guernsey. Feudalism lingers on throughout the Channel Islands. In Guernsey the seigneur of each fief still receives *congé*, 2% of the purchase price of all property sold, which has given problems as the seigneur with the most fiefs is the Sovereign.

Certain property-owners are liable to pay *chef-rente*, a small tax on their homes, and *poulage*, originally two chickens but later converted to a nominal sum. *Quarantaine* used to be 40 eggs, but in 1927 this, too, was converted to a small cash sum as compensation for depriving the seigneur of the use of his land.

At one time the eleventh sheaf of all cereal crops was given to the seigneur as *tithe*, with farmers in a Crown-held fief having to give the twelfth sheaf to the Sovereign; the States took over responsibility for the latter due, and pay a nominal sum to the Crown each year.

Varech, the right of a seigneur with a coastal fief to claim all wrecks on his beach, has long gone, as has *escheat*, the seigneur's right to claim all property in his fief owned by people who die without making a will.

Sark. The first seigneur of Sark, Helier de Carteret, had the power of life or death over his subjects like a monarch of early Medieval times. He could claim each family's tenth child for his own labour; he could claim tithes on the fish catch until 1583; until recently he had a tithe on all corn and wool produced and the monopoly of milling corn; he is the only person on Sark who may own an un-neutered female dog and keep pigeons.

He is still entitled to the *treizième*, one-thirteenth of the selling price of property, and *escheat*, but the latter was last enforced in 1885.

Historic. The first Sovereign to visit Sark since the Norman Conquest, was Queen Elizabeth II, who came in 1957. The event was historic in another respect as it was the first recorded time when a woman – the Dame of Sark, Sibyl Hathaway – paid homage to another woman.

Dame Sibyl said: "Ma Souveraine Dame, je vous rends hommage lige et vous sera foyale et loyale contre tous." The Queen replied: "Nous vous acceptons advouant tous vos légitimes droits et possessions relevant de cette tenure de vous, sauf pareillement à tous nos droits de régalité."

THE CLAMEUR DE HARO

The most unusual and perhaps bizarre relic of feudalism is the Clameur de Haro, still used several times a year around the islands.

It's believed that Haro is a corruption of Rollo, the name of the Viking who created the Dukedom of Normandy. Any of his subjects

Rocquaine Bay has excellent sands below the high-tide shingle.

could appeal to him for help, and it is amazing to find that this appeal can invoke the power of the law more than 1,000 years later.

When an islander believes he or she is being wronged or cheated – for example, if a neighbour threatens his property – the appellant must kneel, hatless, at the site of the alleged offence, and in front of two witnesses shout: "Haro! Haro! Haro! A l'aide, mon Prince, on me fait tort!" – help me, my Prince, somebody's doing me an injustice!

In Guernsey and Alderney he must then recite the Lord's Prayer in French.

Sark demands that the entire cry be in French: "Haro! Haro! Haro! Au nom du Dieu et de la Reine, laissez ce travail sur demande de [the appellant's name] qui vous previent."

The ancient law demands that the alleged threat or injustice must cease immediately until the case is heard, and in the Bailiwick of Guernsey the appellant must then put his case in a written statement to the Bailiff and two jurats within 24 hours.

THE PATOIS

Each bailiwick had its own version of Norman French, the *patois*, each with innumerable local variations, and until recent times it was possible to tell from a Guernseyman's speech in which parish he was born. Nowadays you'll seldom hear the patois, although there is a good chance if you go to Guernsey's West Show. The local languages are not taught in schools and are rapidly dying, with only the *Société Guernesiaise* and its Jersey counterpart checking the haemorrhage.

Here's the National Anthem in the Guernsey patois:

> *Dyu sauve not'Gracieuse Royne,*
> *Vive, vive, not'Noblle Royne,*
> *Dyu sauve la Royne.*
> *Qu'a seit Victorieuse,*
> *Heureuse et Glorieuse,*
> *Long temps sus nous qu'a Raigne,*
> *Dyu sauve la Royne.*

This is by George Métivier, Guernsey's leading poet:

> **Hé! Qu'est donc qui fait chunna?**
> *Aquànd les filles sont gràndettes,*
> *Qu'est qui fait qu'i n's'écàntent pus*
> *A poupines et mariounettes*
> *Et longues lûres à l'ouaîzé blliu?*
> *I n'pensent qu'à ribans, dentelles,*
> *Chapiaux, colrettes et bobans,*
> *A s'attìntaïr et s'faire belles –*
> *Hé! Qu'est donc qui fait chunna?*

The Channel Islands have a great tidal range, hence these steps at Sark's Maseline Harbour.

S'nou tapait sous leux mêzelle,
I n'en faisaient aucùn cas;
Pour ùn regard de leux fidéle,
I s'passraient de tous leux repas!
Quànd nou les baisait p'tites filles,
Il en faisaient le r'fugna;
A-cht-heure, il en voudraient mille –
Hé! Qu'est donc qui fait chunna?

This is a loose translation, sacrificing some accuracy for the sake of rhyme:

Now, what's the cause of that?
When girls are getting into teens,
Why can't they still amuse
Themselves with those old toys and tales
That once they used to choose?
They now think but of frills and lace,
Of ribbons, ties, or hat,
Wherewith their beauty to adorn –
Now, what's the cause of that?

When at their door we used to tap,
Unmoved they would remain;
But now, they'd miss their every meal
To glimpse their favoured swain!
When once we kissed them, little girls,
They feigned refusal flat!
Today they want a thousand more –
Now, what's the cause of that?

Translation by John Linwood Pitts, published 1883.

MOVING IN

Since the early 1960s and the development of the offshore financial services in the main islands, there has been a steady demand from outsiders for homes here, away from the clutches of tax inspectors in Britain and elsewhere.

Guernsey. Guernsey coped with the problem by creating a two-tier housing market; islanders buy in the 'local' market, in which prices are comparable with better-class homes in the south-east of England, but outsiders must trade solely in the 'open' market, holding around 1,800 larger properties whose prices are several times higher than they would be in the local sector. You could say the starting price is £250,000.

With permission, Guerns can put their homes on the open market, but they are then compelled to stay in it, competing with expatriate millionaires; the only advantage is when they plan to move no more, leaving their assets to their children.

The **Fort George** estate south of St Peter Port has been redeveloped as a Millionaires' Row, where some properties have now passed the £1,000,000 mark.

Workers essential to the top end of the island economy, which usually means skilled financiers, have to compete in the open market, while those serving the bottom end, such as catering staff from Portugal, must take lodgings: they may not rent or occupy property in their own name.

Alderney. There is no such pressure on Alderney, where anybody who is a subject of the Sovereign qualifies for residence and can buy a home. In the early 1990s prices started at £70,000 for a two-bed flat in St Anne's, peaking at £450,000. Alderney has limited the number of new houses to five a year, all for locals, and there are strict controls on extending properties, not only because of pressure on space but also because of an acute water shortage.

Sark. If you can find your ideal home on Sark you can buy it and, if it's one of the original 40 holdings, you automatically get a seat in the Chief Pleas. Prices are lower than on Alderney but there are fewer properties available, and many of them are small and have corrugated iron roofing, replacing the thatch of earlier times to reduce the risk of fire.

Jersey. The most difficult island to enter as a resident is Jersey, which not only has the two-tier property market, with prices on the 'open' list well into the million-pound bracket, but also has a selection committee. Until 1986 the States of Jersey admitted 15 wealthy immigrants a year, but as it's now down to five, any aspirant Jerseyman must have several million pounds in liquid assets.

The other islands. Brechou off Sark, Jethou near Herm, and Lihou on Guernsey's west coast, have all been on the market since the war and are in private ownership, usually leasehold; and Burhou, west of Alderney, is a nature reserve.

4: SARNIA'S STORY

Bronze Age to Duke Rollo

THE FIRST PEOPLE TO SETTLE in Guernsey were probably Neolithic (New Stone Age), who may have come from Spain around 3,000BC. Traces of their defensive earth works are still visible around the coast.

Grandmother of the Cemetery. Their best-known relic is La Grand'mère du Chimquière, a human figure carved from granite, probably by rubbing another lump of granite on it for day after day. La Grand'mère has been dated to around 2500–1800BC, and her rudimentary breasts lead us to suppose she was a mother goddess, but the detail on the face and hair are suspected of Roman origin from 100BC–100AD.

Early Christians incorporated pagan relics wherever possible, so La Grand'mère found herself in the cemetery of St Martin's Church until she was moved to form the main gatepost.

From the 18th cent to the early years of this century, the statue became the focus of **witchcraft** and black magic ceremonies, and it was not unusual to see flowers or money laid before her as offerings. A 19th-cent churchwarden who objected to these activities is claimed to have split the stone, but local protests resulted in its repair. Another churchwarden unsympathetic to the old beliefs moved Grandmère to the gateway.

A second female figure of the same era stands in Câtel churchyard, having been found in 1878 under the chancel floor.

Dolmens. Several dolmens (burial chambers built above ground) have survivied around the island, notably **La Varde Dolmen** by the 17th green on L'Ancresse golf course. Guernsey's largest, it is 34ft (11m) long by 13ft (4m) wide, the largest capping stone being 16ft (5m) long and 3ft (1m) thick; imagine primitive men moving it into position. Near the 5th green another burial chamber is claimed to be the most important of its type in western Europe.

The second-largest is the **Hougue de Déhus** or Déhus Dolmen near the Beaucette Marina and with its modern doorway only four feet from the road. Its burial chamber is around 30ft (10m) long by 5ft (1.52m) high, and a spotlight picks out with difficulty the *Gardien du Tombeau*, the tomb's guardian, the carving of a bearded man with bow and arrows. A far-sighted islander bought the dolmen in 1775 for £4.10s (£4.50) to save it from quarrymen, and it's now open daily 0900-sunset, free; parking opposite.

The word *hougue* comes from the Old Norse *Haugr,* meaning 'hillock,' and belongs to the islands' Norman era.

The third-largest dolmen is **Le Creux ès Faies,** the 'Fairy Grotto' – *creux* is Norman French for hollow, cave, cleft – beside the road to Lihou Island and with a parking area beside it. In more recent times the little folk were believed to live here, and had their own tunnel running to **Le Creux des Faies,** another dolmen at Houmets in the north of Câtel.

Follow the coast road north-east to **Le Trépied,** a small dolmen on the top of a rise, associated in the recent past with witchcraft rites. This area is known as **Le Catioroc,** which Victor Hugo claimed to be haunted by the cries of women waiting for their lover, the Devil.

Dolmens on nearby Lihou Island were almost totally destroyed, and those on Herm are barely recognisable. You may find remains of a tomb by Alderney's Fort Tourgis, but the much later Iron Age pottery on Longis Common has more to offer – most of it in the Alderney Museum.

Iron Age. Radio-carbon dating places the site around 500BC, but with indications that it was a long-term settlement. Les Huguettes (or Hougettes), discovered in 1968, has revealed a potters' workshop and

Le Trépied, looking west to Lihou Island.

The Déhus Dolmen has some enormous ceiling stones. How did primitive man manoeuvre them into position?

settlement, with large amounts of broken pots, as well as some Bronze Age tweezers and razors.

Excavations at **Vale Castle** in Guernsey revealed a hill fort dating to around 550BC, but the largest Iron Age earthworks, at **Jerbourg,** were begun at the end of the Stone Age and were still being strengthened in the 14th cent. Then the Germans built their Strassbourg artillery battery on the site.

A few longswords, spearheads and beads have been found in small tombs around **Le Catioroc** and classed as La Téne type; most are in the Guernsey Museum. Evidence of Iron Age salt pans has been found on Herm, and in 1718 some finely-worked horse decorations came to light in Sark, but have since been lost.

Romans. The Romans came around 150AD, stayed 250 years, but left very little trace. **The Nunnery** on Alderney, also known as the Château de Longis for its location on Longis Bay, is the best-preserved building from the times, but the most dramatic discovery was the 3rd-cent shipwreck which Dr Margaret Rule raised from the sea bed near the mouth of St Peter Port harbour; it will eventually go on display.

The Romans are credited with naming the main islands *Sarnia, Riduna,* and *Caecarea,* today known as Guernsey, Alderney and Jersey, the *–ey* ending, meaning 'island,' being a Viking addition.

Dark Ages. The Dark Ages, following the collapse of the Roman Empire, were particularly dark in the Channel Islands. **St Magliore**

came to Sark around 550, using the island as a base for sending friars to the other isles, and when he died in 587 his body was taken to Lihou and on to Paris. At the same time, **St Helier** arrived in Jersey, surviving as a hermit until his murder in 555.

Vikings. History begins again around 814 with the coming of the Viking raiders, who seized footholds on the Seine and the Loire. In 911 Rollo, the chief of the Seine group, was powerful enough to take control of the Caen area from its Breton inhabitants and have it ceded to him by Charles the Simple of France at the Treaty of St Clair-sur-Epte. This was the beginning of the **Duchy of Normandy,** but it took Rollo's son, William Longsword, to add the Cotentin peninsula in 933, presumably including the Channel Islands. Traces of a Viking longhouse have been found at Cobo in Guernsey and in Old St, St Helier, but there was probably very little settlement. The main influences were the introduction of Norman law, *Le Grand Coutumier,* which was far ahead of its time and included the *Clameur de Haro;* and of feudalism.

In the 10th cent, Normandy was ruled by a succession of colourful dukes: Richard I, the Fearless; Richard II, the Good; another Richard who was just III; Robert the Devil; and William II, the Bastard.

Throne of England. Bastard William had a good claim to the Throne of England as he was first cousin once removed to King Edward the Confessor, who had died earlier in 1066. Harold Godwineson took the throne by popular acclaim, but soon had to defend his realm against a Norse invasion, at the Battle of Stamford Bridge.

Duke William II saw his chance, and on 28 September he landed 8,000 men at Pevensey, Sussex, to claim the Crown of England. Sixteen days later he defeated Harold on what are now the grounds of Battle Abbey, and became King William I. Normandy, with the Channel Islands, had defeated England.

5: LES ILES NORMANDES

Guernesey, Sercq and Aurigny

THE JOINT KINGDOM saw some anomalies in the Channel Islands, whose seigneurs paid their taxes to Rouen in Normandy while being ruled from William's new capital, London. Before the conquest of England, William had leased Sark and Alderney to the monks of Montebourg, the Mont St Michel in the Gulf of St Malo, and Herm to the Augustinian monks of Cherbourg; and the Bishop of Coutances appointed all priests. When William the Conqueror died in 1087, his elder sons split the territory, William Rufus taking the throne of England while Robert retained the dukedom of Normandy. Jersey stayed true to Normandy, while Guernsey kept its allegiance to England.

Clameur. There's an interesting anecdote to the Conqueror's burial. He was killed while attacking Mantes, down-Seine from Paris, and was to be buried at St Stephen's Abbey, which he had built in Caen. A freeman, whose house had been demolished to make way for the abbey, raised the *Clameur de Haro* for compensation, which was paid before the funeral could proceed.

Treaty of Caen. Four years later, William II and Duke Robert 'Short Hose' agreed at Caen that whoever survived the other should reunite the territories, but when William was killed in the New Forest by an unknown archer in 1100, the pair's younger brother Henry seized the throne of England. Henry I, 'the Lion of Justice,' had the support of the English nobility which allowed him to resist his brother Robert, who came back to claim the throne.

Henry proved his injustice by invading Normandy in 1104, defeating Robert at Tinchebrai (between Avranches and Caen) in 1106, and imprisoning him for his remaining 28 years. Jersey was back under the English Crown, while Henry continued his conquests, forcing Louis the Fat of France to surrender Brittany and Maine.

Confusion. Henry's son William was drowned in a shipwreck in 1120, believed to be on the **Casquets** reef west of Alderney. Henry, deprived of a direct heir, therefore persuaded the Great Council to acknowledge his daughter Matilda as his successor but she, already the widow of the German emperor, married Geoffrey Plantagenet of

"This is the BBC..." Guernsey folk followed the progress of World War Two on radio sets that they hid from the Germans.

Anjou and so reinforced the French complication.

When Henry died of a fever in Normandy, his nephew Stephen – son of William I's daughter Adela and the Count of Blois – urged the Great Council to give the Crown of England to him rather than to Matilda, and in 1135 he became King Stephen.

Normandy, with the Normandy Isles, deserted Stephen and pledged loyalty to the true heir, Matilda, and to her husband, Geoffrey of Anjou. Now, Geoffrey and Matilda had a son, another Henry – Henry Plantagenet – who was not only heir to the Duchy of Normandy but also (because he married Eleanor of Aquitaine, the divorced wife of France's Louis VII) was the Sovereign of Aquitaine and Gascony: the total was more than half of modern France.

Stephen died of a heart attack at Dover in October 1154, having been forced to agree to Henry Plantagenet as his successor.

Vast realms. When Henry II succeeded to the English throne he had vast possessions, stretching from the Cheviot Hills to the Pyrenees, from Killarney to the Cevennes. And somewhere in the middle were the insignificant Normandy Isles.

Henry and Eleanor had seven children, the oldest dying in 1183. The thirdborn, Richard of Aquitaine, joined King Philip Augustus of France six years later in manoeuvring Henry's downfall; Henry escaped, but died of a fever in the Château de Chinon in 1189, leaving Richard of Aquitaine to become Richard I, the Lionheart. Richard spent only 10 months of his 10-year reign in England (see *Discover*

Cyprus for his exploits in the Crusades), but his treachery was rewarded when the soldiers of Philip II of France shot him with an arrow.

John Lackland. Richard's brother John became king in 1199 – but all his French subjects except those in Normandy and Aquitaine preferred his nephew, Arthur. Philip II of France saw his opportunity and snatched Normandy from him in 1204, but never touched the Normandy Isles.

Divided loyalty. The islanders now had a stark choice to make: should they remain loyal to the Crown of England, which still represented the Duchy of Normandy, or should they go with France? For most the decision was easy: England had the bigger fleet, and King John personally pledged that the islands' ancient laws and privileges would be maintained. But families who held lands in the islands and on the French mainland had the worst choice, usually deciding to forfeit the smaller part of their estates.

The Iles Normandes therefore opted for the English Crown, where they have remained ever since, except for brief interludes under French, German and Flemish occupation. The islanders' choosing to stay with England refutes any claims that the English conquered or colonised the islands, and makes them unique within the British Commonwealth. But henceforth they were to be known as Les Iles Anglo-Normandes.

Enemy shores. Very soon the defences were begun. The man who had recently been Governor of Rouen, Pierre de Préaux, moved to Guernsey and began building **Castle Cornet** in 1206. He was barely in time, for the first serious French raid came in 1214. By 1244 the castle had eight towers, and under Governor Geoffrey de Lucy (1224-6) was strengthened further, with records showing that de Lucy spent £66 19s 1d (95.5p) on the work.

There is no proof of the legend which claims that the French captured Guernsey in 1295 and held it briefly, but it is accepted that a Welshman named Owen or Evan led French troops who landed from Vazon Bay in 1373. The 800-strong Guernsey Militia, founded in 1337, fell back to Castle Cornet or Vale Castle where Owen besieged them for a short while before sailing away.

Jerbourg. Edward III became king in 1327, after his father was murdered with a red-hot poker in his anus. The next year he recognised Robert the Bruce as King of Scotland, thereby worrying Guernseymen who knew Scotland's main ally was France. They asked Edward for another castle, where they could take refuge with their livestock, as Castle Cornet was on an island. Edward ordered the building of Gyrbourg (Jerbourg) Castle, but the place was far from complete when the Hundred Years War began in 1338.

Guernsey captured. The Marshal of France, Sir Robert Bertram,

Lord of Bricquebec, seized Guernsey, Alderney and Sark almost at once. In retaliation, Edward III assumed the title of King of France with no hope of achieving it, and adopted the motto *Dieu et mon Droit*. In 1340 he defeated the real King of France at the Battle of Sluys (Netherlands), then sailed down-Channel and in August began the recapture of the Guernsey Bailiwick. By October he had achieved it, except for Castle Cornet which held out for Philip VI for another five years.

The French took Guernsey again early in 1356, but their defeat at Poitiers in September led to the **Treaty of Calais** and their abandoning all claim to the islands. They would very soon render the treaty worthless.

The Guernsey people finished Jerbourg Castle, which has long since been destroyed and, in return for their loyalty, Edward confirmed their customs and privileges, which almost every monarch has done down to the present.

Jersey. In 1373 the French seized Jersey, except for Gorey Castle, but held the island for only a few weeks.

Meanwhile, the monks of Mont St Michel in France still occupied Sark. Henry V (1413-22) ousted them at the start of his reign, and saw that Guernsey or England provided the priests in future. But Sark had no proper harbour, inadequate drinking water, and was rather inhospitable; it would give trouble in later years.

Those were the good old days! A main road in Sark at the height of the tourist season.

Joan of Arc. In 1415 Henry V defeated the French on a soggy October cornfield at Azincourt (Agincourt), a tiny village between Arras and Boulogne-sur-Mer, and once again took control of northern France – except Mont St Michel – thereby relieving for the moment the threat of attack on the Channel Islands. But three years later, in the village of Domrémy-la-Pucelle, Meuse, a girl was born who would change the fortunes of France. Jeanne d'Arc, believing God was her personal ally, drove the English from Orléans in 1429 but died on the stake before France could regain Normandy, which it did in 1450. Once more, the Iles Anglo-Normandes stayed with England, which now held just Calais on the French mainland.

Alderney. But what of Alderney? Duke William of Normandy had loaned the island to the abbot of Mont St Michel back in 1042, with the Bishop of Coutances taking the lease from 1057; Alderney had stayed under Coutances for some 300 years yet was governed by the King's Court of six jurats, a *prevôt* (sheriff), and other officers. The Crown owned the windmill, but the bishopric owned the watermill, both of them serving the farmers who worked the 450 acres (180ha) of arable land in the Blaye (*blé* is French for 'wheat'), roughly where the airfield is today. Alderney, the island closest to France, was an anomaly even down to its agriculture: medieval strip cultivation was standard, yet feudalism had never been introduced.

Wars of the Roses. Scarcely had the Hundred Years War with France ended in 1453, when the Wars of the Roses erupted in England (1455-86), putting Lancastrians against Yorkists.

Royal treachery. The Yorkist Edward IV (1461-83) was married to Margaret of Anjou, a French princess and a Lancastrian supporter. Margaret's allegiances understandably inclined a little towards her native land so that when she rewarded her cousin Pierre de Brézé, Compte de Maulevrier and Grand Sénéschal of France, for his help in her quandary over divided loyalties, she did it by *giving* him the entire Channel Islands, which he occupied forthwith as Lord of the Isles.

The people of les Iles Anglo-Normandes, rightly fearing they would lose their independence under the French Crown, supported the Seigneur of St Ouen ('san wenn'), Jersey, one Philippe de Carteret, who seized Gorey Castle – by then known as Mont Orgueil, 'Mount Pride' – by a landward attack in 1468 while the English fleet bombarded it from the sea.

Bailiwick. Liberated Jersey was created as a separate Bailiwick, and when the English freed Guernsey soon after, it became a second bailiwick; it was from this moment that the islands began developing their distinctive political characters.

Papal Bull. At the end of the Wars of the Roses, Edward IV and Louis XI of France resurrected the Treaty of Calais by agreeing that the Iles Anglo-Normandes should be neutral territory, and Pope Sixtus IV issued a Bull (a command) to that effect, which was displayed in the cathedrals of London, Canterbury, Salisbury, Nantes, St Pol de Léon, and Tréguier (both in Brittany), and St Peter Port church. The Bull proclaimed the islands and their waters 'as far as the sight of man goes' to be neutral in war, on pain of excommunication, and it remained official if not effective until 1689.

Despite the islands' owing allegiance to the English Crown, the Bishop of Coutances continued to appoint the parish priests until 1499, when Pope Alexander VI transferred the honour to Salisbury and later to Winchester, but in the following year a new rector on Jersey made certain that both bishops had authorised his appointment. The Bishop of Coutances finally lost his hold on Alderney, which the English Crown then leased to Edward Portman; was it coincidental that he was from Salisbury?

Catholicism fades. Henry VIII (1509-47) threatened the actions of both popes when he attacked Catholic principles by demanding a divorce from his queen Catherine of Aragon, which he effected in 1533. The Channel Islanders, who had seen many Huguenots fleeing from persecution in France and had listened to the ideas coming from Martin Luther, supported Henry and by 1547 had scrapped all outward evidence of their own Catholic faith: by 1560 the last of the wayside crosses, still typical of northern France, had gone, and the islanders were practising a sober Calvinist faith with fun and laughter on Sunday punishable by a jail sentence.

But perhaps Catholicism was merely in hiding, for in 1559 the Governor of Guernsey still clung to his faith, and in that year his Catholic son George Chamberlain was granted the lease of Alderney.

Alderney. Henry VIII had begun fortifying Alderney in 1546, the last full year of his reign, with the idea of turning it into a naval base to counter the possible threat from nearby Cherbourg, yet the Papal Bull proclaiming the islands' independence was still nominally in force. Alderney's crude harbour at that time was Longis Bay on the east coast, protected only by the ruins of the Roman *Castrum Longini,* now called the Nunnery. Henry began building the larger fort of *Les Murs de Haut,* 'the Upper Walls,' but work ceased in 1554. It was the Victorians who completed the Upper Walls, but by then it was called **Essex Castle** from the Earl of Essex who bought the governorship from John Chamberlain in 1591.

Sark recolonised. The French Captain Bruel occupied uninhabited Sark in 1549 with 400 troops and built several forts, but the men lost interest and gradually went home. Nine years later some Fleming adventurers seized the island and offered it as a wedding present to Mary I, who had married Philip of Spain in 1554; Mary never replied.

The Creux ès Faies mixes medieval legend with ancient historic fact.

The disenchanted Flemings destroyed the forts and abandoned the unwanted island.

Unwanted? In 1565 Helier de Carteret, a Presbyterian Jerseyman, offered to recolonise Sark in the name of the new monarch Queen Elizabeth. She accepted.

Elizabeth granted de Carteret 'and his herds' the island in perpetuity, yet when he arrived with his wife and servants he found 40 or 50 farmers had moved in with their livestock and were running a moderate export trade in meat and grain. He imposed his authority on the peasantry, drew a map of the island, and presented it to the Queen, who granted him in return a *Fief Haubert,* a 'Royal Fief,' backed up by six cannon, but those seen on the clifftops today came much later. De Carteret's charter obliged him to maintain on the island 'forty men at least, our subjects' – their descendants today sit on the Chief Pleas – and to supply to the Crown, on demand, a horseman wearing a coat of mail, a *haubert,* known today as a 'hauberk.'

English Civil War. For generations past, Parliament had been gradually increasing its authority in England and Wales, although it still had no say in the Channel Islands. By the time Charles I was crowned in 1625 (1633 in Scotland), Parliament was too powerful for Royal comfort, and in 1642 the smouldering antagonism became the flames of civil war, leading eventually to Charles's execution in Whitehall on 30 January 1649. Meanwhile, with the monarchy under threat, where would Channel Islanders' loyalty lie?

Vazon Bay offers splendid sands for the children, 'vraic' for the smallholder, and rocks for low-tide crab-hunting.

Alderney had little choice as its Lieutenant-Governor was Captain Nicholas Ling, commander of a Parliamentary garrison and of the Alderney Militia – he held the latter post until he died in 1679, aged 80. Sark's seigneur and Sir Philippe de Carteret in Jersey supported the monarchy.

Castle Cornet on Guernsey was loyal to the Crown but, surprisingly, the people of the island forgot their allegiance and backed the Parliamentarians.

The English Lieutenant-Governor, Sir Peter Osborne, moved into Castle Cornet and defended it for the next eight years against Parliamentary attack; the story is told that during this difference of opinion he fired 10,000 shot into St Peter Port, but another version claims it was 30,000. Sir Peter was forced to surrender on 19 December 1651, the last person to haul down the standard of Charles I.

Seven years earlier, Parliament's troops had invaded Jersey and begun an interminable siege of the two main castles. The defenders were the first in the realm to acknowledge the succession of Charles II, on 17 February 1649, only 18 days after Charles I's death; they surrendered four days before Guernsey, on 15 December 1651.

Knitting. After the Restoration, the islands entered a period of relative peace, broken only by a brief French attack on Jersey. The fishermen discovered the Newfoundland Banks and their wealth of cod; other islanders expanded the knitting industry which had, allegedly, supplied the stockings that Mary Queen of Scots wore at her execution in 1587. A century later, the earnings from knitting were so great that men were neglecting the harvest to take up their needles. Britain's Industrial Revolution killed most of the trade, but knitted guernseys and jerseys still find a slot in the market. And John Wesley went to Guernsey and Alderney to reinforce his Methodism.

Napoleon. The French were back in 1789, this time as refugees from their revolution. Many of the aristocracy settled in the islands, becoming loyal subjects of the British Crown and bequeathing a new influx of surnames as well as some of the smarter manor houses. But the greatest legacy of the times is the large number of round towers standing on lonely beaches and in every small bay, from the northern tip of Guernsey to the low-tide rocks off southern Jersey – but not on the smaller islands. They were built to withstand yet another attack from France, this time from Napoleon, and they predated by a very few years the much larger towers that line the English coast from Suffolk to Sussex. As *these* were based on a defensive work built on Cape Mortella, Corsica, they came to be known as **martello towers.**

Tomatoes. Guernsey discovered the glasshouse in 1792, before the end of the Napoleonic threat, and produced grapes for the table until 1865 when tomatoes began replacing them. Soon the island was supporting acres of glass and developing a lucrative export market to Britain, killed by cheaper Dutch fruit after World War Two. At its peak the industry would employ 75% of the working population.

Sark silver. Somebody discovered silver on Little Sark in the early 19th cent, leading to the formation of the Hope Mining Company in 1834, with seigneur Ernest le Pelley as chief shareholder. The island's population in the 1831 census was 543, but a decade later it stood at 790, its highest ever, due to the presence of mineworkers.

The boat carrying the first silver to England, diverted to Guernsey so the captain could visit his sick wife, and was wrecked with the loss of cargo and crew. On the same day, seawater flooded the mine's lower galleries, killing all hope for the Hope Mining Co. The seigneur avoided bankruptcy by selling his Fief Haubert to Mrs T. G. Collings, whose descendant is the present seigneur. If there was a happy side to the story, it was the beginning of the tourist industry as Guernsey folk came over to see the mineshafts, which still survive on Little Sark.

Queen Victoria. The Victorians decided that Alderney must be fortified, as it had missed the martello tower panic. Not only was Henry VIII's Murs de Haut completed, but the Victorians added 13 other forts which cost £260,000 and were never used in anger.

Then there was the breakwater. Napoleon had gone, but the British were so concerned about the breakwater protecting Cherbourg that they decided Alderney must have one large enough to shelter a sizeable fleet. The work was a major undertaking on such a small island: St Anne was expanded to house the workers; a paddle steamer began a regular link with Guernsey to bring in their supplies, and so started the tourist industry; tourism needed hotels, Scott's being the first; and a railway was needed to haul the stone from quarries in the east of the island, which brought more tourists – and, on two occasions, Queen Victoria herself.

Alderney Railway. It was the only standard-gauge track ever laid in the islands and is now the only survivor, running a tourist service between harbour and quarry. The railways on Jersey and Guernsey? They were built in the 1870s, but went out of business in the 1920s in the face of competition from the buses.

But the Alderney breakwater was a failure. It extended 4,827ft (1,471m) into deep water, but could not withstand the ferocity of the Atlantic storms. It survives at half its original length, its landward end a safeguard for Braye Harbour but its seaward end a menace to all boats using that harbour. It even defied the *Wehrmacht* which was desperately eager to make the islands impregnable during the five years of German Occupation in World War Two.

The only surviving railway in the Channel Islands has a strange mixture of locomotives and rolling stock – but steam is available.

6: HITLER'S FORTRESS ISLES

Die Ärmelkanalinseln

THE BRITISH GOVERNMENT, responsible for the defence of the Channel Islands, decided in 1925 that Guernsey and Jersey were so vulnerable to attack from France by air and sea that to defend them adequately may be impossible, and to defend them inadequately would be to expose the islanders to unnecessary attack. Therefore they would be demilitarised. British troops soon left Jersey, but they stayed in Guernsey until 1939.

By June 1940, with the Nazi *Wehrmacht* getting closer each day, Whitehall couldn't decide whether to uphold the 1925 decision or to send in troops. The two Lieutenant-Governors were appealing for arms, and on Alderney the Machine Gun Training Centre personnel were being withdrawn to Guernsey with such speed that the islanders began to panic.

Whitehall farce. The lack of leadership and contradictory advice from London continued for several vital weeks, leaving the three States – including Alderney – having to look after themselves. As Hitler's troops drew nearer, States officials asked themselves whether they had been abandoned, or merely forgotten.

Finally, on 15 June 1940, Whitehall and Parliament decided that the islands would not be defended, and the Lieutenant-Governors, the last administrators to go, left on 21 June. The civil evacuation, carried out amid panic, took off virtually every one of the 1,100 people on Alderney and 20,202 from the main islands, plus those who travelled independently by mail boat. People abandoned cars and cycles at the harbour in the rush to escape, yet the next week growers sent 300,000 baskets of tomatoes to England.

Only on Sark where Dame Sibyl Hathaway maintained feudal authority, did nobody opt for evacuation: the 471 people would stay.

With the evacuation and demilitarisation complete, one Government faction wanted to publicise the fact to prevent German bombing raids, but another wanted to suppress it as the Nazis would construe it as an invitation to invade.

Invasion. The *Luftwaffe* bombed both main islands on the 28th and the *Oberkommando der Wehrmacht*, the OKW, was ready for its elaborate invasion plans in which Stuka dive bombers and torpedo boats were to precede the main landing force of six batallions – but the entire operation was made obsolete on 30 June when the pilot of an observation plane landed on Guernsey's aerodrome and learned the truth: the islands were defenceless.

That evening, Junkers transport planes flew in a platoon of Luftwaffe soldiers and the occupation of Guernsey had begun. The following day, 1 July, was Jersey's turn, and hours later two planes landed on Alderney, cleared the barbed wire from the airstrip, and declared the island occupied. On 3 July a small detachment sailed from St Peter Port to Sark, and the occupation was complete, although none of the islands signed a formal declaration of surrender.

'Anger.' Britain had bungled the defence; it then proceeded to make matters worse by staging several commando-type operations, such as *Ambassador, Anger* and *Parker*, all aimed at Guernsey, which couldn't help the islanders and merely antagonised the Germans. *Operation Tomato*, planned to hit all the islands in September 1940, was cancelled. Nor was it practical for the civilian population to operate a resistance movement with organised sabotage, as there was nowhere to hide.

At first, life continued as before, with little interference. The States passed legislation, which had to be approved by the Kommandant instead of the King; church services and public entertainment were allowed; and it wasn't an offence to hear the British National Anthem on the radio.

Insular life. But soon problems began to appear. British markets for Guernsey tomatoes and Jersey potatoes vanished, and unemployment became a major problem. Communication with the outside world was extremely difficult, and people needed a good reason before they could get permission to travel between the main islands.

Hitler, meanwhile, had grand plans for the *Ärmelkanal Inseln,* the 'Sleeve Channel Islands.' While France would be governed by the French after the war (but under German supervision), the Channel Islands would never be handed back to a defeated Britain. They were to become outposts of the German Reich, providing holiday homes for the *Herrenvolk.*

But in the short term the Ärmelkanal Inseln, the first and only British territory to fall to the Wehrmacht, were to become the most heavily-defended section of the Atlantic Wall, although in practical terms they were more of a liability than an asset to the German war machine. Massive concrete gun emplacements went up at almost every headland, but the largest weapons were the four 305mm-bore (1ft exactly) naval guns located at Le Frie Baton in St Saviour, Guernsey, and camouflaged to look like houses; the underground barracks absorbed 45,000cu m of concrete and had rooms for 400 men.

These guns began life on a Russian battleship which the Germans seized in 1918, then returned it to Russia where it was broken up in 1935. The guns went on to Bizerta (Tunisia) and in 1939 were en route to Finland when the Germans captured them again.

The **Occupation Museum** pictures of one of these guns but, for real drama, visitors should have seen the ammunition stored in tunnels under the parish church during the war, which is obviously impossible.

Concrete. Tunnels and concrete dominated the defences. By January 1944, 484,000 cubic metres of concrete had been used in the islands, while the rest of Hitler's Atlantic Wall, stretching from north Germany to the Bay of Biscay, used 6,100,000cu m. By the same date, 244,000cu m of rock had been dug away, almost as much as the 255,000cu m removed for the entire mainland part of the wall. To appreciate 484,000cu m, imagine a solid block of concrete 78.5m (257ft) in every dimension.

The **Military Underground Hospital** in St Lawrence, Jersey, was dug by civilian slave labour, including women and children, and involved cutting away 14,000 tons – 10,000cu m – of rock.

Land mines. Hitler supplemented his concrete by laying land mines on the beaches: 67,000 in Jersey, 68,000 in Guernsey, 37,000 on Alderney and 4,500 on Sark. He compounded his megalomania on defence by having up to 37,000 troops permanently garrisonned on the islands guarding a civilian population of similar size, and at one time he had 2,426 troops on Alderney, more than twice the peacetime population.

Guernseyman Frank Stroobant recorded his experiences of occupation and deportation in *One Man's War*, beginning with light-hearted instances such as when he served condemned meat to German troops in his harbourside restaurant. When cooking fat vanished from the market he nearly gassed himself by frying chips in linseed oil, having decided that motor oil was too dangerous. Stroobant found a publisher, the Guernsey Press, in 1967, and his book has been in print ever since.

Stroobant comments that the Germans at first believed the islanders to be unwilling subjects of British colonialism, but changed their opinion after the loss of HMS *Charybdis* early in the war. When the Germans held a military funeral for the 19 British bodies washed ashore, 'scarcely an islander was absent from the service' and 721 wreaths were sent.

The various museums show the more serious side of life under occupation, such as the epitaph to *Louis Berrier, charged with having released a pigeon with a message for England. He was therefore sentenced to death for espionage by the Court Martial and shot on 2nd August 1941.* Usually the islanders had no option but passive

Did the wearer of this Organization Todt identification tag live to see the war's end?

resistance, such as by painting BRITISH VICTORY IS CERTAIN on road signs. The Germans countered this by painting their own 'V' signs.

Food shortages. Gradually and relentlessly, hunger began to rule people's lives, especially after the Allies' invasion of Normandy in 1944, which cut off all supplies from France. The islanders roasted and crushed lupin seeds, acorns, parsnips and sugar beet in their search for a coffee substitute; parsnips, pea pods, bramble leaves and carrots served for tea; dried elderberries became sultanas; coltsfoot, bramble, and sweet chestnut leaves served as tobacco; and potatoes were milled for flour. The Germans imposed stringent restrictions on fishing, leading to yet another substitute: macaroni and anchovy sauce boiled until stiff, then fried.

In the final days even the Germans were near starvation, as shown by the last menu for the garrison in Jersey's Elizabeth Castle:

Morgen: 100gm Brot.
Mittag: Suppe Nudeln; Goulasch.
Abend: Eintopf; Wurst, 80gm; Butter, 35gm; Kaffee; Brot.

Morning: 3.7oz bread.
Midday: Noodle soup, goulash.
Evening: Stew, 2.75oz sausage, 1.25oz butter; coffee; bread.

Black market. Midway through the war, most shops were open for only a few hours daily but, beyond the business centres, the black market was in operation, with goods being sold for British money, not the unpopular Occupation Reichsmarks. Butter sold for £2 a pound (90p kg) and meat was 15/– a pound (34p kg), at a time when £3 was a good weekly wage. Eggs were 2/– (10p) each, a hundredweight (50kg) of wheat was worth £25, and a farm horse sold for £500.

The 319th German Infantry Division which came in 1941 brought more than 600 horses, mostly taken from French farms. After the Normandy landings the 4oz (113gm) weekly meat ration ceased, and soon civilians and soldiers alike were eating the horses; only 308 were left when the islands were liberated. They were sold to the islanders, the last one dying in 1968.

Bureaucracy. To prevent the troops joining the black market, every purchase had to be backed by a licence from the *Feldkommandantur*, even for one shirt button. At another time, all boats in Guernsey had to be taken to St Peter Port at short notice: it wasn't enough to report their existence. The order included everything that floated, including canoes and the punt from the ornamental pond of Sausmarez Manor.

Escapes. There was only one successful escape, that of Denis Vibert who crossed the Channel in 1941 in a 9ft (2.75m) open boat from St Aubin's Bay, Jersey, taking three days to reach a minefield off Portland Bill, where he was picked up.

Deportation. The greatest exodus of civilians came in 1942 when 1,182 British-born islanders were deported to Germany, many at only a day's notice. A year earlier, Britain had asked that German residents in Iran should be handed over; Hitler's response was to demand British residents in the Channel Islands be sent to Germany – but on a ten-for-one basis. The order was quietly forgotten until the Swiss Government revivied memories with a suggestion for the exchange of wounded prisoners.

Organization Todt. The deported Britons received reasonable treatment, as far as life in a concentration camp can be considered reasonable, but back in the islands several thousand Organization Todt workers were cruelly abused. Dr Fritz Todt had devised his organisation before the war, and now he used it to bring in starving survivors of the Spanish Civil War, French Jews, plus Ukrainians who, allegedly, walked barefoot across Europe, and others who had become dregs of humanity. It was coincidence that *Tod* is German for 'death,' but eyewitness accounts claim that hundreds, if not thousands, of OT workers starved to death or were murdered – although hard proof is difficult to establish.

Concentration camp. Solomon Steckoll claimed in his book *The Alderney Death Camp* (Granada, 1982) that of the four camps for slave labourers on Alderney, the one called Sylt, beside the airport runway, was as much an extermination camp as Dachau, Sachsenhausen and Belsen, although it lacked gas chambers and incinerators. The notorious SS – *Schutzstaffel*, 'protection squad' – whose officers guarded Sylt, had some very special German prisoners under their control: 120 *Wehrmacht* ('Army') and two SS officers, many of whom had been decorated by Hitler in person, but who had been convicted of treason and were awaiting 'special punishment' after the war.

The other camps on Alderney were Heligoland by Fort Tourgis, Borkum between St Anne and Essex Castle, and Nordeney near Fort Albert, all named from islands off north Germany. Major-General Count Rudolf von Schmettow, the Kommandant of the occupied islands, confirmed up to 3,000 OT workers were on Alderney in 1943, and 13,000 were elsewhere, and it is on record that the entire Organization Todt was withdrawn soon after the Normandy landings, as there was no further point in building concrete bunkers. Hitler personally ordered the SS out to avoid the traitorous officers being captured by the Allies, and today almost nothing remains on the ground of the only extermination camp to be built on British soil. And Steckoll insists there was a major cover-up after the war to prevent news of Sylt leaking to the public.

Bypassed. Meanwhile, Operation Overlord, the invasion of Europe, bypassed the Channel Islands for several reasons: the manpower and material necessary for their liberation would be too much; there would be major damage to property; the islands were not strategic; and the islanders were on reasonable terms with the occupiers.

Starvation. As the last winter of the war approached, and the Allies headed for Paris and the Rhine, some high-ranking German officers tried to persuade Hitler to evacuate all Channel Island civilians to France. After the German loss of St Malo this changed to appeals to ask the British to evacuate the islanders, or to send them food. The British Government approved the mercy rations but Prime Minister Winston Churchill refused to risk British food going to any of the 28,500 German troops instead of to the 62,000 remaining islanders.

"Let 'em starve," he wrote. "No fighting. They can rot at their leisure." He meant the Wehrmacht but, as Germany would not relinquish the Ärmelkanal Inseln, his comments applied to all 90,500 people.

Surrender. Adolf Hitler's death was announced on 1 May, 1945, heralding the German surrender. On 8 May Churchill had the more comforting words "...and our dear Channel Islands will be freed today," but it was early on 9 May when the Royal Navy entered St Peter Port, and a few hours later when Jersey was officially free. Peace was two days old before British troops managed to reach Sark, where the Dame had to be left in charge of 275 prisoners for almost another week. Of the 2,832 prisoners captured on Alderney all but 500 were taken off when the island was officially liberated on 16 May, the very last German outpost to surrender. The war in Europe was at an end.

For a full account read *The German Occupation of the Channel Islands*, by Dr Charles Cruikshank, published by the Guernsey Press and continually in print.

The 'town church' of St Peter Port is at a busy road junction (above),
but Vale Church (below) is tranquil.

The Germans added a gun emplacement to Fort Richmond (above) but didn't spoil this view from Icart Point (below).

7: ISLES OF LEGEND

Little islands; little folk

BEWARE TCHICO; he's evil. Tchico is a spectral dog, quite often black but sometimes invisible save for his big, staring eyes. He roams the islands by night and is a warning of bad news to come. Sometimes known as *La Bête de la Tour,* the 'beast of the tower,' he roamed the old Tower Hill, site of many executions in St Peter Port.

The strange thing is that the legend of Tchico, the dog with big eyes, is found in many places in Britain and to a lesser degree in France; there's a Sarkese Tchico who wanders across La Coupée by night.

Bailiff's Cross. A small stone bearing a cross marks the site where Gaultier de la Salle, a highwayman, is supposed to have stopped to take Holy Communion before being hanged. Confusingly, the stone is at the crossroads known as Bailiff's Cross; more confusingly, there are several versions of the story. One claims that a bailiff oppressed his people beyond the point of endurance, hanging one man for a crime that he himself had committed – but justice was done and the bailiff was hanged here.

Another version says that the innocent victim had received a Royal pardon, so the bailiff was hanged instead, while a third variation says that Gaultier de la Salle tried to have his neighbour condemned so he could have sole use of a well; when the truth came out, it was Gaultier who hanged.

Chevauchage. In feudal times the peasants had their bonds of allegiance relaxed for one day a year, when they ran around the parishes kissing every female they saw, even if she were the seigneur's own wife. At the end of the hectic *chevauchage* in Torteval, the peasants gathered at **La Folie,** a shallow circular trench about 15ft (3m) across, cut into the greensward. They sat on the outer rim, dangling their feet in the trench, and were in effect sitting at a table covered with a green cloth – the grass. And here the seigneur would serve them with a meal...or was it all a fairy tale?

Perhaps it was. Another story tells of *pions,* youths dressed in white but with black caps, who came with officials inspecting the highways. Here, at **La Table des Pions** they sat on a ring of boulders to eat their lunch; there's no mention of the trench. Yet another version says that the grooms of the horsemen involved in the *chevauchage* or *chevauchée* sat here on the boulders, their feet in the trench while they ate. The truth is somewhere here: remember that *pion* means 'lowly man, pawn,' and *chevauchée* is 'horse-riding.' Now look for La Table near the car park at Pleinmont Point, and make up your own mind.

It is a fact that various seigneurs at various times held extraordinary power over their serfs, such as the right to take to bed any young woman they fancied. Most seigneurs whose fiefs ran down to the beach had the right to claim all wreckage, and an unknown number have lit large fires on dangerous coasts on stormy nights – not to serve as warnings, but to infer the safety of a harbour.

Witchcraft. Belief in witches and witchcraft in the Middle Ages was rife in the islands, as indeed it was in England and France. Guernsey has the unenviable reputation of having convicted, on average, one witch per year for 150 years, while England, with a much greater population, convicted 2,000 in the same time. Guernsey's chief witch-hunter was Bailiff Amice de Carteret who ordered the execution of 35 witches and the banishing of 19 others between 1601 and 1635, showing that even the mightiest families in the community fell under the influence of sorcery.

The last witchcraft trial in Guernsey began on 29 January 1914 and resulted in Amy Henrietta Queripel being sentenced to eight days' hard labour.

The witches' favourite meeting-places for 'sabbats' were **Rocquaine Castle,** now the Fort Grey Maritime Museum, and **Le Catioroc,** usually on Friday evenings – which coincides with the beginning of the Jewish *shabbat,* or holy day. The women are alleged to have rubbed *le verjus au diable,* literally 'the Devil's own sour grapes' on their skin to give them magical powers.

Guernsey's tallest standing stone, the 11ft (3.5m) **Longue Rocque,** not far from Le Catioroc, began life as a cricket bat used by the little folk, who must have had superhuman strength to move it, far less play with it.

In the early 1880s a mortal man from St Saviour wanting to rid himself of his late father's *mauvais livres,* 'bad books' containing spells, threw them on the fire. They put the flames out. He dropped them down a well; it dried up. Finally, on advice, he buried them in their own element at the bottom of a pile of farmyard manure, where the ammonia destroyed them.

Burnt at the stake. Legend tells of the Guernsey woman in her 80s sentenced to death for witchcraft in 1640. On her way to be burned at the stake in the *Vallée de Misère,* a giant raven flew over. She threw it a length of black cord, which it seized, lifting her away as she hung onto the other end. A youth threw his staff at the bird, so making it release the cord and drop the witch, who was duly burned. But the boy died within the year, choked during his sleep. Provided you don't ask where the old woman found the cord, the only problem with this story is that there was no witchcraft execution in Guernsey in 1640.

Devil's names. In the old days, people believed that a mixed marriage – a Guern with a Jersey person – was doomed to failure, and Jersey folk said of a blazing summer sunset that "Guernsey's burning." Nicknames – 'Devil's names' – were common, with Guernsey folk being called donkeys, Jersey people toads, Alderney folk cows, and Sarkese crows, all names being in the appropriate patois.

In addition, Guerns had nicknames for each other depending on which parish they lived in. Câtel and Torteval folk were donkeys (they were that already for being Guerns); Forest folk were drones; St Martin's were ray fish; St Peter in the Wood's were beetles, St Saviour's ants; and Vale folk were cockchafers.

Probably the strangest story concerns Mr Hocart, whose field on the Vale and L'Ancresse boundary held the ancient stone called **La Rocque qui Sonne,** 'The Ringing Rock.' When he planned to demolish it, people warned him not to, but he went ahead and included some of the shattered stone in his new house. When he was ready to move in, the house burned down, killing two servants. He shipped some of the stone to England, in two vessels: both sank. He moved to Alderney, but his home there burned down. Finally, he sailed back to Guernsey, but the ship's rigging fell on his head and killed him.

They started with grapes, moved to tomatoes, and experimented with kiwi fruit. This Guernsey glasshouse now grows roses for the cut-flower trade.

Torteval's parish church is the newest in Guernsey, but its bell is the oldest in the Channel Islands.

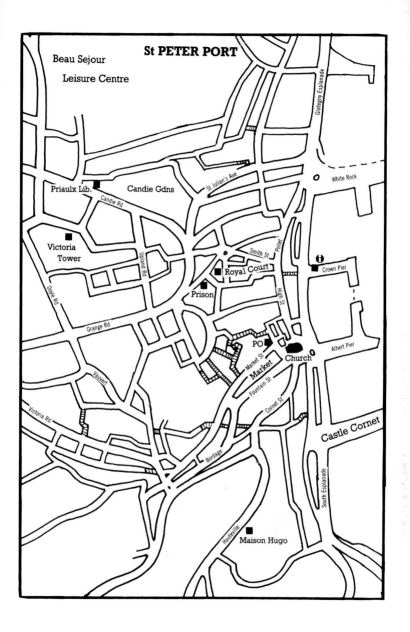

St PETER PORT

Beau Sejour
Leisure Centre

Priaulx Lib.   Candie Gdns

Candie Rd

Glategny Esplanade

St Julian's Ave

White Rock

Victoria
Tower

Upland Rd

Smith St

Pollet

Royal Court

Crown Pier

Doyle Rd

Prison

High St

Grange Rd

PO

Albert Pier

Vauvert

Market St

Market

Church

Victoria Rd

Fountain St

Cornet St

Castle Cornet

Bordage

South Esplanade

Haitzville

Maison Hugo

53

8: GUERNSEY

And Lihou

ALL GUERNS AGREE that St Peter Port, which they call 'the town,' is the prettiest community in the entire islands. Most visitors agree – after all, Guernsey puts its light industry and power station out of the way at St Sampson, while Jersey's St Helier has its power station on the edge of town.

Nonetheless, St Peter Port is charming, with its picturesque waterfront and marina, framed by the town church to the south and by the 100ft (30m) **Victoria Tower** on the skyline: built in 1848 to commemorate Queen Victoria's visit in 1846, it also served as a signalling station to Alderney.

Wine. The town began as a fishing village, but the presence of Castle Cornet from the 13th cent prompted it to become the island's main port, and two small piers enclosed a sheltered harbour. From the 14th cent this tax-free town began importing wines from Bordeaux, sending them on to England when the market was favourable. This led to smuggling – the Guerns called it 'free trade' – which, with the officially-approved privateering, created much of the early wealth and explains some of the town's fine Georgian buildings.

The Harbour. The original piers, renamed Victoria (now Crown) and Albert, couldn't serve the steamships and in 1853 **Castle Pier** began creeping out towards Castle Cornet, making the link in 1859. Scouring began at once, so the pier had to be extended seawards into a breakwater. At the same time **St Julian's Pier** extended seaward from the clocktower, forming the present harbour; on this jetty you might see the memorial plaque to the 33 islanders (*source, Cruikshank; others claim 23*) killed in the only German air raid, on 28 June 1940. The 1893 extension added 220ft (61m), and in 1896 another 60ft were added, known as **White Rock Pier,** from where the Sark ferries sail. In the 1980s the area to the north was enclosed to form the 20-acre (8ha) **North Beach Marina,** holding 800 yachts and 1,000 parked cars.

Castle Cornet. The castle's story is told in chapter 5, but here's a summary:

1206, Pierre de Préaux began building the castle;

1214, first serious French attack repulsed;

1337, besieged briefly by Welshman leading French troops;

1338, Guernsey and Cornet seized by French under Bricquebec;

1340, Edward III recaptures Guernsey but not Cornet;

1345, Cornet liberated;

1356-7, recaptured by French; Cornet extended and reinforced under Elizabeth I;

1642-'49, Civil Wars, Guernsey goes Parliamentarian but Cornet is last Royalist stronghold, surrendering 15 December 1651;

1672, lightning strike causes explosion which destroys keep; governors cease living in Cornet.

The castle is now open daily Apr-Oct 1030-1730, for £4. It's a large, rambling fortification that has seen military occupation or action for nine centuries, including numerous small additions dating from the German occupation.

Cornet today holds six separate museums, the high entry fee covering them all: the **Maritime Museum** has exhibits from the Gallo-Roman boat which archaeologists have named *Asterix*, to the Royal National Lifeboat Institution; the **Hatton Gallery** is home to many portraits and paintings; the **Royal Guernsey Militia Museum** has memorabilia of this force from 1743 and lists the governors since 1177, but its main exhibit is the sword given to Maj. Gen. Thomas Dundas who strengthened the defences in anticipation of France's declaration of war against England in 1793 after Louis XVI had been beheaded.

The **Main Guard Museum**'s eight rooms cover military and naval history from the 16th cent to the German occupation, including the Guernsey Falcon, a six-pound cannon cast in 1550 and presented to the State of Massachusetts, USA, in 1921. It was returned in 1956. The **201 Squadron Museum** remembers 'Guernsey's Own' squadron of the RAF, and the **Armoury** holds weapons from the Civil War to the present.

Prison. The castle incorporated the original island prison, its jailer originally being called the *Portier du Château*. Early portiers were well-paid at 12d (5p) a day from Crown funds, but as they lived in town they couldn't reach the castle on its islet in stormy weather. The resulting suffering and starvation of prisoners led to numerous escapes from sheer necessity, as well as from increased opportunity, and eventually a petition for a new prison went to the King in Council. After deliberating for four years he gave his assent in 1803, and the prison was built in St James's St between 1811 and 1815 for £11,000. Of its 19 cells, two were for women, five for debtors, eight for felons, and four for the connétables' convicts.

The castle's Carey Tower was a special prison for three jurats during the Civil War, but they escaped as the writ for their execution was being prepared.

Castle Cornet ceased to be of military use at the end of World War Two, and in 1945 George VI presented it to the people of Guernsey, so beginning its role as a major tourist attraction. Soon after, the ancient ceremony of firing the noonday gun was reintroduced, and two men in red coats now terrify the gulls in the harbour every weekday at the stroke of 12.

Railways. Back on the Esplanade, you're handy for the Guernseybus terminal. Earlier visitors may remember this firm trading as the Guernsey Railway Company, showing its origins. The first railway had been planned in 1845, to run from town up an impossibly steep hill and go on to Perelle Bay. By 1871 the idea was a plausible standard-gauge line from St Peter Port to St Sampson and L'Ancresse Bay, where a deep-water harbour was planned.

The first stretch of line was in use by 1878, but it was soon obvious that Guernsey lacked the necessary passenger-miles to make the venture pay, and within the decade it collapsed. In 1889 the newly-formed Guernsey Railway Company revived the line, and its small steam locos and electric cars ran until 1934, by which time the parent company had transferred its loyalty to the motor bus.

German railways. But that wasn't the end of railways in Guernsey. The *Wehrmacht* relaid the lines on 90cm gauge and extended them down the west coast to L'Erée, in order to transport the thousands of tons of stone and concrete for the Atlantic Wall; they planned another line from town across the hilly south, to Torteval.

A reminder of five grim years: the Occupation Museum near Fôret Church.

The German *Eisenbahn* went through back gardens by the score, pierced boundary walls by the hundred, and at Richmond went through a greenhouse. A few packing sheds and the odd house had to come down, and in the 1970s guests at the now-gone Hotel Les Carterets near Saline Bay, sat on the course of the line whenever they dined.

Aquarium and Military Museum. Go south along the esplanade and you eventually reach the entrance to a tunnel begun in 1861 – the date over the entrance reads 1864 – to take a road to Soldiers' Bay. It now holds the **Guernsey Aquarium,** open daily 1000-sunset (~1545 in winter), and displaying sea and freshwater fish from European and tropical waters. Nearby, in a German World War Two tunnel, is **La Vallette Underground Military Museum,** a new venture which holds relics from 1914 to 1945 and is open daily 1000-1800.

Fort George. On the hilltop above stands millionaires' row, properly known as Fort George. Begun in 1780, this large complex to replace Castle Cornet as the main defence, had a Citadel, the smaller Fort Irwin, and the batteries called Kent, Adolphus, Charlotte and Clarence. The Germans armed it, but Allied bombers destroyed it in 1944 just before the Normandy landings. After the liberation, the War Office sold the ruins to the States of Guernsey who sold it to a British developer who built the luxury homes which now feature on the 'open' property market – hence Millionaires' Row.

The nearest beach and bathing place for the soldiers of Fort George is at the foot of the cliff. It's still called **Soldiers' Bay,** but access is only via steps and the beach is pebbly.

Town Church. Back along the Esplanade, the next feature of interest is St Peter's Church, 'Sancti Petri de Portu.' The original was wood, probably the building that William of Normandy gave to the Abbot of Marmoutier, near Tours, in 1048; he had already given St Sampson, St Martin, St Mary's at Torteval, and Holy Trinity at Forest to Mont St Michel.

The church, known as the 'Cathedral of the Channel Islands,' grew over the centuries, stone replacing timber. The chancel is 12th cent, and the south chapel was added in 1462, beginning 13 years of work which transformed the building. In 1483 came the order from Pope Sixtus IV granting the islands neutrality, with a copy of the text displayed at St Peter's. In 1414 the church came under the patronage of the English Crown, but the Bishop of Coutances appointed the clergy and collected the tithes until 1548.

The spire was restored in 1721, the bells recast in 1736 and again in 1913, and the clock added in 1781. In 1886 the interior was realigned as the original seating faced all directions, while the windows are modern, replacing glass blown out during the Occupation. A plaque on the wall remembers Guernseyman Maj-Gen Sir Isaac Brock of the

British Army who became administrator of Upper Canada, today's Ontario.

Opposite the church, Cornet St has the Guernsey National Trust headquarters at **No 26,** the oldest house in town, dating from the 17th cent and now restored in the style of a shop of 1900. Sweets and souvenirs are on sale Apr-mid Oct 1000-1600, while the GNT ofice is upstairs.

Victor Hugo. Cornet St rises steeply to Hauteville, 'High Town,' and Guernsey's most popular attraction for French visitors, **Hauteville House,** where French writer Victor Hugo lived in exile from 1855 to 1870.

Born in Besançon in 1802, the son of a major in Bonaparte's army, he married Adèle Foucher in 1822. Nine years later he wrote his masterpiece, *Nôtre Dame de Paris,* featuring the hunchback Quasimodo and translated into English as *The Hunchback of Notre Dame*; soon he received the Legion d'Honneur and was elected to the Académie Française. In 1845 he became a peer and, when Louis-Philippe was deposed in 1848, he found himself in the Assemblée Nationale.

But trouble was coming. His liberal politics suggested he exile himself, first to Brussels and then in 1852 to Jersey with his mistress Juliette Drouet, whom he met when she acted in his play *Lucrèce Borgia* in 1833. When Jersey expelled him he came to St Peter Port where Mrs Drouet already lived; they remained lovers until Hugo's death in Paris in 1885.

Hugo wrote *Les Misérables* in Guernsey, his best-known work in Britain following the West End stage version, but his furniture and tapestries were bought from the proceeds of privateering and he refashioned them to furnish the four-storey house in its present elaborate style. He said: *"J'ai manqué ma vocation; j'etais né pour être décorateur."* He also said, less truthfully, that the Channel Islands were *morceaux de France tombés à la mer et ramassés par l'Angleterre.* ("I missed my vocation; I was born to be a decorator;" pieces of France fallen into the sea and gathered by England.)

The ground floor's two drawing rooms have a tapestry from Queen Christina of Sweden and a statue from the Doge's Palace in Venice while a pillar in the hall has carved scenes of Nôtre Dame de Paris; the first floor features a heavily-carved oak gallery; the second holds the Hugo family rooms and his study, where he wrote *Les Misérables* in 1862, and in 1866 *Les Travailleurs de la Mer*, translated as *Toilers of the Sea,* and other works – all while standing at his desk. The house, now owned by the City of Paris, is open Apr-Sep 1000-1130, 1400-1630, with 15-person guided tours every 45 minutes.

Water. Go back to the church and up Fountain St for the site of the old fountain and water-powered sawmills and corn mills, fed by a small reservoir near the present Mansell St, in turn fed by a stream flowing down today's Colborne Rd. The town's expansion and the need for improved hygiene removed all this activity.

Old Market. But some of the old ways have returned with the revival of the Old Guernsey Market, where else but in Market St, May-Sep on Thurs afternoons. Traditional craft wares are on sale, with some of the stallholders in 19th-cent costume.

The States approved a covered market in 1726, and a private-enterprise meat market received its Order in Council in 1777, resulting in the Old Market hall being built in 1780, with the Assembly Rooms above it. By 1822 the butchers' stalls had moved across Market St, making way for greengrocers. The buildings are still in use but the Assembly Rooms, where John Wesley preached in 1787, are now the **Guille-Allès Library,** of 50,000 books, open Mon-Sat 0910-1700.

Town Gates. None of the six town gates, supposedly built in 1350 on Edward III's orders, has survived, but in 1700 granite boulders went up to mark their locations; look for them near the Town Church, in upper Cornet St, in Smith St and Fountain St. There is even some doubt whether the gates were built, leaving the granite pillars as markers for what might have been. Known as *Barrières de la Ville,* the gates – or the pillars – were not only for the protection of the town but also marked its boundaries – and that had a major significance. The law of primogeniture, locally called *préciput*, applied in rural areas, dictating that the firstborn son inherited the family lands intact. It did

The impressive Royal Court House on Rue du Manoir.

not apply within the town, presumably because there were no farms, but as St Peter Port expanded beyond its walls, *préciput* was pushed back and farmholdings within the boundaries were split up. The law of primogeniture was rescinded, and *préciput* was abolished in 1954.

Just north of Mansell St is **Nôtre Dame du Rosaire,** a French Catholic church amid cobbled alleys. Wander west to 25-27 Victoria Rd for **Guernsey Toys,** which has been making and exporting soft toys since the 1960s; it's open Mon-Fri 0900-1300, 1400-1700, plus Sat morn in summer.

Oldest PO box. Going from Guernsey Toys on foot, Cordier Hill Steps leads to Allez St (*allez* is French for 'go!') and Union St. And here, Letter Box 1 proudly stands in a front garden, not only the first Post Office collection box in the Channel Islands, but one of the oldest in the British Isles.

At the end of Union St, Saumarez St leads north to Elizabeth College, or south to **Constitution Steps,** whose 146 stairs are reminiscent of the Rock of Gibraltar or, considering their original name was Les Escaliers de Mont Gibel, a French hilltop town. There are several stepped streets in old St Peter Port; and others which retain their old French name alongside the present English version, but the majority of bilingual streets are in Jersey's St Helier.

Elizabeth College, founded by Good Queen Bess in 1563, had become a second-rate school by 1826, when the present mock-tudor structure was built. The college which, with the Victoria Tower, dominates the skyline, now has an excellent reputation.

Due east, at the top of St James St, the old church of St James the Less, built in 1815 to give British troops the chance to hear a church service in English, was reopened as the **Concert Hall** in 1985, but it also features exhibitions, film shows and lectures. St James St leads into the medieval town, nowadays the administrative heart as well. If you pass the Old Prison on the right, built 1811-'15 for £11,000 and, at St James's lower end, you turn right into Manor Place (Rue du Manoir), you'll see the **Royal Court House,** built in 1799 and now the seat of the island government as well as the court house for that rare major trial; tourists may sit in the visitors' gallery when the States is in session, and go into the Greffe, an office which holds all the charters granted since 1394.

Ann's Place, opposite Manor Pl, has the former Government House, now a hotel, facing a sunken garden where St Paul's Methodist Church stood until 1972, on the site of La Maison Carrée (The Square House), once the home of Admiral Lord de Saumarez, spelt without a middle 's.'

And that brings you out to the junction of Candie Rd and St Julian's Ave, which plunges steeply to the harbour. If you're on foot, turn into the no-entry-for-cars Candie Rd for **Candie Gardens,** part of the

It looks cute, but the trolleybus is really a modern vehicle in disguise. The '1931' number plate adds a clever touch.

Candie Estate which Oswald Priaulx presented to the island in 1887. The States decided in 1898 to create the gardens, and they're now one of the town's summer horticultural show-pieces, as well as holding statues of Queen Victoria and Victor Hugo. Candie House became the **Priaulx Library,** a treasurehouse of 25,000 books dating back to the 15th cent and including almost everything published on the Channel Islands. It's open Mon-Sat 0930-1700 for reference, but members of La Société Guernesiase, which has its headquarters nearby, may borrow material.

The old bandstand near Victor Hugo's statue has become a restaurant, incorporated in the **Guernsey Museum and Art Gallery,** now in its purpose-built home which opened in 1978, and which won the national Museum of the Year award in 1979. The building uses the bandstand's design as a recurrent theme, and shows the island's history from prehistoric times to the present, with emphasis on Guernsey's famous folk and its crafts and industries. Open daily 1030-1730 (~1630 winter), except Xmas-New Year.

The Osmond Priaulx who founded the library was a descendant of Pierre de Préaux who founded Castle Cornet. **Castle Carey,** by the way, is an elegant 19th-cent house built for William Carey, whose collection of Oriental and European porcelain is in the Art Gallery. The house is on Les Côtils, 'Steep Slopes,' near Beauregard ('Beautiful View') Lane, so you can expect some splendid panoramas of the town and harbour, with Sark on the skyline.

Beau Séjour. A footpath leads from near Castle Carey, through Cambridge Park, to the Beau Séjour Leisure Centre, a large sports and entertainment complex open to residents and visitors. Beau Séjour – 'pleasant stay' – which opened in 1976 in the grounds of a large house, has almost everything you could wish for in entertainment, from the island's only cinema to the ability to present a major pop concert, with discos, dances, one-armed bandits, television lounges and bars as standard. Or try your hand at bridge, chess, darts, scrabble or whist. You're a sports enthusiast? Then you have access to a heated swim-pool with water slides, gymnasia, saunas, and you may try badminton, squash, hockey, netball, crazy golf, tennis on seven courts, or go roller skating, canoeing, fencing, trampolining or synchronised swimming.

The on-site shops sell books and souvenirs, snacks and sweets, and three times a year the Guernsey Amateur Dramatic and Operatic Society puts on shows. The centre is open daily 0900-2300, with generous terms for holiday membership.

Super Fred. The Super Fantastically Reliable Electronic Device, alias Super Fred, chooses the winners in the Channel Islands Lottery, which pays around £50,000 as its first prize up to 20 times a year, the Guernsey share of the profits going to finance Beau Séjour.

Banknotes. As you go back to our starting-place you may notice near The Quay a plaque to Thomas Moullin, born in Guernsey in 1813, who became a founder member of Pearl Assurance in 1864. Not far away is the *Thomas de la Rue* pub, named from the man born in Forest in 1793. He was apprenticed to a printer in St Peter Port in 1802, and later moved to London to set up his own business. Today the firm of Thomas de la Rue prints banknotes for governments around the world – including those of Guernsey and Jersey.

AROUND THE ISLAND – clockwise

St MARTIN

St Martin has Guernsey's longest stretch of rugged coastline, holding some of the island's favourite bays. Here they are:

Fermain Bay, named from the Breton word for 'sturdy rock,' has a steep road access with *cars banned,* and it's also reached from the cliff pathway. During the summer, boats carry passengers from Albert Pier, St Peter Port, five times a day, returning 30 minutes later. The top of the beach is steep and shingly, but there's good flat sand at low water, and le Grand Creux, an impressive cave. Martello tower, café, toilets.

Alternatively, come along the cliff path from La Vallette by the Aquarium, which gives glimpses of the old walls of Fort George and

The 'Grandmother of the Cemetery' stands forlornly at the gate to St Martin's Church.

continues on to Jerbourg and, eventually, Pleinmont in the west.

Bec du Nez and **Marble Bay** are reached only along this path, or from other paths from the road to Jerbourg. Marble Bay, originally *Pied du Mur*, 'foot of the wall,' reveals relics of the old Jerbourg Castle.

Telegraph Bay on the heel of the Jerbourg peninsula takes its name from the cable which ran to Jersey, but its original name was Vaux Bêtes, 'Valley of Beasts.'

The Germans destroyed the original 1825-built **Doyle Column** on **Jerbourg Point** in 1944 because it helped the RAF locate their 'Strassbourg' gun emplacement. The rebuilt momument on the peninsula's highest point again commemorates Sir John Doyle, Lieutenant-Governor from 1803 to 1813, whose achievements included building Fort George, the *true* Martello towers at Fort Grey, Fort Saumarez (no 's') and Fort Hommet, and draining the marshy land of Braye du Valle on the Vale–St Sampson boundary, which made Vale parish almost an island.

Offshore, the **Peastacks** are an impressive chain of four pillars, once known as *Les Tas de Pois d'Amont,* a roundabout way of saying the same thing. Fishermen used to salute one rock, *Le Petit Bonhomme d'Andrilot,* 'The Simple Man of Andrilot.'

Petit Port, accessible down 230 steps, has some of the best sands on the island but should be avoided in a south-westerly wind. Café at top of steps.

There's a road down to **Moulin Huet,** pronounced 'moo-lan wet,' tracing the course of a stream, but parking spaces are limited and are not directly by the beach. Shingle gives way to perfect sand, and there are several caves. It's possible to walk to Petit Port at low tide but you're advised not to risk it. Legend claims that Cradle Rock, in the bay, is where three local girls fell asleep and were caught by the flood tide: don't follow their fatal example. The Lion and Dog rocks are on the western edge of this picturesque bay.

At the top of the road you may see on your left the remains of a windmill owned by the de Sausmarez family. The name, Moulin Huet, comes from the water mill that once straddled the stream much lower.

A road leads to **Saint's Bay,** probably named from rocks said to resemble saints. The top of the beach is shingle, with sand at low water; there's deep water around the little harbour, and limited parking space between a martello tower and a monument to a seigneur of Blancheland who helped to pay for the harbour.

Icart Point has a good car park, toilets, and snacks, as well as splendid views; the coastal pathway comes near the car park, giving easy access if one of your party wants, for example, to walk down to Saint's Bay or on to Petit Bôt.

This footpath and its allied steps is your only access to **Le Jaonnet Bay,** from where, at low tide, you can walk to **La Bette Bay** and explore its large Dog's Cave – but watch that tide!

Petit Bôt, 'putty bow', on the boundary with Forest, has a narrow lane for access and limited parking. Again, shingle gives way to sand. The Germans destroyed the upper watermill here, but the lower one is now a café; toilets are nearby.

Let's wander into Forest to look at **Portelet Bay,** the last one on the south coast and accessible only by footpath – but not at high tide.

Church. Inland, the parish church of St Martin de la Bellouse – or Bellieuse – is known for its menhir, la Grand'mère du Chimquière, who stands guard by the gate – her story is in chapter 4. The present church was begun around 1225, with the nave, tower and chancel being completed by 1250. The south porch, built around 1520, was the meeting-place of the *Douzaine,* the parish council, until 1869.

Highest point. A kilometer west, along Forest Rd, stands the Haut Nez – 'High Nose' – water tower, crowning the highest land in Guernsey, 342ft (104m) above mean sea level. But south-east lie the attractions of Sausmarez Manor.

Sausmarez Manor. Be careful of spelling when you think of Sausmarez Manor, as it's spelled with an S in the middle; Saumarez Park in Câtel, former home of Admiral Saumarez and now home to the Folk Museum, has no S.

The four-storey Manor, one of the stateliest of the island homes, stands on the site of a Norman house and was much restored in Regency and Victorian times as its architecture shows. Captain Philip

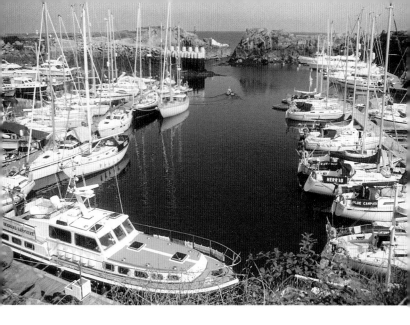

A contrast in coves: Beaucette Marina (above) and Grand Grève, Sark (below).

The island-hopper's view of Alderney's overlarge breakwater (above) contrasts with a glimpse of the ferry leaving Sark's Maseline Harbour (below).

Sausmarez sailed with Admiral George Anson in 1740 to raid Spanish ships in the Pacific. All the fleet except Anson's flagship, *Centurion*, was lost around Cape Horn, and the *Centurion* sailed around the world to limp home almost four years later – but with £500,000 worth of plunder from Manila in her holds, the richest prize ever taken at sea. Some of the proceeds came to Capt Sausmarez enabling the family to regain Sausmarez Manor in 1748; it had passed to the Andros family in 1557 when Seigneur George de Sausmarez died without an heir.

The manor house now holds a splendid array of treasures from the past seven centuries, including the log of the *Centurion*'s historic voyage, James II's wedding suit, and a wide display of tapestries, paintings and furniture, all of which survived the German Occupation partly because the seigneur, Sir Havilland de Sausmarez, had not installed electricity: the Germans therefore dropped their plans to convert the manor into a hospital. The Dolls' House Collection which came over from Lihou Island in 1992 has model homes built from 1830 to modern times; the Tudor Barn has a **Model Railway** on 00-gauge with at least eight trains working, and an outdoor 7.25in (18.4cm) gauge railway takes you on a tour of the grounds.

The **manor** is open for guided tours May-Sep, Wed-Fri and bank hols, 1030-1200, 1430-1630; the **railway** is open daily except Feb 1000-1800.

Moulin Huet Pottery. At La Fosse, on the road down to Moulin Huet Bay is a pottery that has been producing clay pots, mugs, vases and other items for many years, and has become a popular attraction. Watch the potters at work, then buy some of their wares; alternatively, commission something and call back for it in a few days. Open Mon-Sat 0900-1700 year round; Sun 1000-1600 May-Oct.

St ANDREW

Underground Hospital. Among the attractions of the only parish without a coastline, the German Underground Hospital is now an innocuous place open Apr-Sep daily 1000-1200, 1400-1700, but its story is the most horrible to emerge from the war in the Channel Islands, except for the atrocities in Alderney's Lager Sylt.

If you have never experienced the horrors of war and want to sample some of its suffering, then come inside. And afterwards, visit the tunnel under St Saviour's church. Even so, there is no way you can recapture the fear, the hatred, the hunger, the desolation, the hopelessness, of total war.

The slave labourers of the Organisation Todt who dug out these tunnels lived with these emotions every day, and most died with them. As they collapsed at their labours their bodies were thrown into the wet concrete of the floors and walls: some of the unfinished side

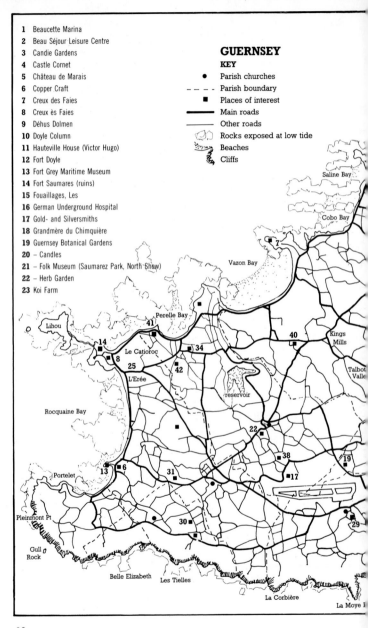

1   Beaucette Marina
2   Beau Séjour Leisure Centre
3   Candie Gardens
4   Castle Cornet
5   Château de Marais
6   Copper Craft
7   Creux des Faies
8   Creux ès Faies
9   Déhus Dolmen
10 Doyle Column
11 Hauteville House (Victor Hugo)
12 Fort Doyle
13 Fort Grey Maritime Museum
14 Fort Saumares (ruins)
15 Fouaillages, Les
16 German Underground Hospital
17 Gold- and Silversmiths
18 Grandmère du Chimquière
19 Guernsey Botanical Gardens
20 – Candles
21 – Folk Museum (Saumarez Park, North Show)
22 – Herb Garden
23 Koi Farm

GUERNSEY

KEY

●   Parish churches
– – –   Parish boundary
■   Places of interest
━━━   Main roads
───   Other roads
〰   Rocks exposed at low tide
〰   Beaches
〰   Cliffs

Saline Bay

Cobo Bay

Vazon Bay

Perelle Bay

Lihou

Kings Mills

Talbot Valle

reservoir

Le Catioroc

L'Erée

Rocquaine Bay

Portelet

Pleinmont Pt

Gull Rock

Belle Elizabeth   Les Tielles

La Corbière

La Moye

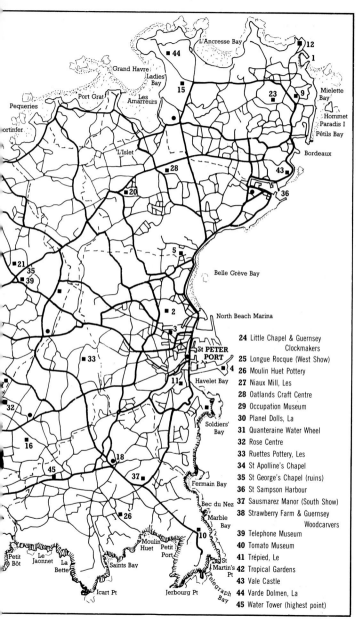

24 Little Chapel & Guernsey
    Clockmakers
25 Longue Rocque (West Show)
26 Moulin Huet Pottery
27 Niaux Mill, Les
28 Oatlands Craft Centre
29 Occupation Museum
30 Planel Dolls, La
31 Quanteraine Water Wheel
32 Rose Centre
33 Ruettes Pottery, Les
34 St Apolline's Chapel
35 St George's Chapel (ruins)
36 St Sampson Harbour
37 Sausmarez Manor (South Show)
38 Strawberry Farm & Guernsey
    Woodcarvers
39 Telephone Museum
40 Tomato Museum
41 Trépied, Le
42 Tropical Gardens
43 Vale Castle
44 Varde Dolmen, La
45 Water Tower (highest point)

The Little Chapel is tiny and unconsecrated, yet it attracts many visitors.

tunnels have this ghastly moment of history re-created with wax models and appropriate sound-effects.

The work lasted 3½ years, in which time 60,000 tons of rock was moved, creating more than 1.2 miles (2km) of passages with a floorspace of 75,000sq ft (7,000sq m). Originally the hospital was planned to hold 500 patients, but it eventually stored thousands of tons of ammunition for months, and saw medical service for only six weeks, from the Normandy landings in June 1940 until the Allies' advance put the hospital out of Germany's reach. It was no great loss as its patients, deprived of sunlight, looked like corpses when they were discharged.

Little Chapel. The rival attraction is the Little Chapel at Vauxbelets, claimed to be the smallest in the world; it's 16ft (4.8m) to the top of its spire and can comfortably hold six people. The work of Brother Déodat Antoine, a De La Salle monk, it's based on the grotto and Church of Ste Bernadette at Lourdes and is the third such chapel. Déodat began the first in 1914 and destroyed it as soon as he had finished. The second one stood until 1923, when he demolished that and began this one. Illness forced his return to France in 1939, shortly before the war, leaving Brother Cephas to complete this chapel, which was mainly a matter of decorating it, inside and out, with tiny fragments of pottery and chinaware. Look for the tiles from Mallorca, Douglas (Isle of Man), Lincoln Cathedral, part of a George IV Coronation mug, and several dozen ormer shells.

The chapel, still owned by De La Salle, is open at any reasonable time and, while it's not consecrated, it has received a blessing from a Bishop of Portsmouth. The large building behind it, which was the monastery, is now a language school.

Ormers. Ormers? These are large bivalve shellfish, *haliotis tuberculata,* or *oreille de mer,* 'sea ear,' in French, at the northern limit of their range and just holding on in the wild – yet records claim that 20,000 were taken on one day in 1841. The States of Guernsey financed an ormer farm which started harvesting in 1988, despite the need to cook the mollusc for 24 hours before eating – and then only on the day of the new moon and the following day, in January and February.

Guernsey Clockmakers. The Guernsey Clockmakers business shares the Little Chapel site, making elegant wood housings for grandfather clocks, wall barometers, and similar objects which it exports worldwide, although the machinery usually comes from Germany. You can watch the carvers at work behind a glass screen year round, Mon-Fri, 0830-1730.

Rose Centre. A little to the north is the Rose Centre where these shrubs are grown under glass for cut bloom, most of which is sold at New Covent Garden or by retail mail-order, with the Royal Family among the customers. A video explains the process of growing roses, while computers do the job of controlling the glasshouse environment. Open daily Mar-Oct, 1000-1700.

Church. The 12th-cent church of St André de la Pommeraye, 'St Andrew of the Apple Orchard,' was originally, in Latin, *Ecclesia Sancti Andreae de Putente Pomeria,* meaning that the orchard was on a gradient – which is obvious. It is one of the smallest churches in Guernsey, but vastly bigger than the Little Chapel which draws far more visitors. The apple orchard has gone.

Zoo. So has the zoo. In its place is the **Guernsey Botanical Gardens,** which opened in July 1992 using some of the zoo's aviaries for its collection of finches and parakeets. The grounds are splendid and colourful, and the enterprise makes its living by selling plants, seeds, and some fruit – there are cumquats in the citrus house. If you want information sheets on Guernsey's flora, including its medicinal plants, then come here. There's also a children's playground, gift shop, and restaurant, with the car park down the road. Open daily from 0930.

The zoo was run by a charitable trust which is continuing its breeding programme in other premises not open to the public.

There's a pottery – Les Ruettes – in the lane of the same name north of Bailiff's Cross, where three or four potters make old-style oven-to-table ware using local clay and ash. Open daily 0930-1730.

FOREST

Forest, also known as Forêt, has cliffs that are second in grandeur only to those of St Martin, and the coastal path provides good viewpoints to walkers. Access down to the sea is confined to **La Moye** by Moye Pt, where a tiny harbour has timber skids for hauling small fishing boats out of the water for the winter, and to the **Havre de Bon Repos,** the 'Haven of Good Rest' under La Corbière Pt, but any vessel that moored here in bad weather would find the 'rest' would be permanent. The lower part of the unofficial path is also a bit hazardous.

West of Moye Pt is **Le Gouffre,** 'The Gulf,' a rugged cleft which truly warrants the description of dramatic; this was where Mrs Guille, wife of the co-founder of the Guille-Allès Library, fell to her death. And almost on the boundary with St Saviour is **La Creux Mahie,** probably Guernsey's biggest sea cave, 188ft (57m) into the rock, by 60ft (18m) wide. The entrance is small, so the cave is dark as well as being dangerous, as there have been roof falls. Keep out.

Church. Inland, the church of Ste Marguérite de la Forêt stands in a small community known as Le Bourg. The nave, tower and chancel are 13th cent, as is St Martin's church, and both have their towers near the centre. In England, north doors were used mainly at baptisms, kept open to allow the Devil to flee as he lost another soul to Christ, but here the north door was originally for the women and children, with the men using the south door. Now everybody enters from the north, where musical instruments are on display, mementos of the days before 1868 when the organ was installed.

Boulders at the south-east corner infer the church may have been built on the site of a pagan dolmen, and the circular churchyard hints that it was an ancient burial ground.

Occupation Museum. The Occupation Museum is in a low cottage almost behind the church, but the façade belies the extent of the exhibits. The museum not only has big objects such as guns and vehicles, but it details the grim years of occupation with forms, newspapers, documents, permits, and orders written by Kommandant von Schmettow.

There is a large display of weapons and small arms, another of German communications equipment, and an 'occupation kitchen' showing what the islanders were forced to eat in late 1944 while they carefully tuned a crystal radio to catch the BBC. Open daily Apr-Oct 1000-1700; Sun, Tues, Thur, Nov-Mar 1000-1630.

TORTEVAL

Torteval's main attraction is its cliffs, not as high as those further east, but no less rugged in their grandeur. The stubby peninsula of Les Tielles reveals a rugged shelf of rock stretching seaward at low

La Coupée links Sark and Little Sark along a razorback ridge.

tide, and from the footpath to the west you may see a natural arch. Rue de Mont Hérault leads down from the main road to the old Mont Hérault watch-house, now showing its age. It's actually in St Pierre du Bois parish, which splits Torteval, Guernsey's smallest, into two.

East, a track leads down to Belle Elizabeth, a headland with a cave. Elizabeth is supposed to be a girl who threw herself from the cliffs after her parents forbade her to marry the man of her choice. West, back in Torteval, there's the rugged **Baie de la Forge** with a splendid souffleur (natural blow-hole) which performs two hours into the flood tide, especially with an onshore wind.

The next watch-house, the 'Haunted House' of Victor Hugo's *Toilers of the Sea*, was a victim of the German Occupation, only a few ruins remaining. The scenery is at its most rugged here, with the headland of La Congrelle; the German fortress sitting on L'Aigle, 'The Eagle;' the dramatic beauty of Gull Rock; and **Les Hanois** lighthouse two miles offshore. *Hanois* – 'han-wah' – is Celtic for 'agony,' which scores of wrecked seamen experienced before the lighthouse was built in 1862.

Around Pleinmont Point, the character changes rapidly as the cliffs drop away and the coast swings around to **Fort Pézèries,** an 18th-cent defence still in reasonable repair. This is the end of the rugged south coast; ahead lie the larger and shallower bays of the west, with a busy road lying just over the sea wall. The sand near the top of the beaches is usually good enough for building castles, but low tide reveals vast rock plateaux.

Church. Torteval has the newest church in Guernsey, built in 1816 at States expense to replace the original, which the parishioners had been unable to maintain. St Philippe's simple round tower is topped by the island's biggest spire, and inside is the oldest bell in the Channel Islands, cast in France in 1432. The cemetery has a strange headstone, to the brothers Walter de la Mare and Bertie de la Mare, both killed on 1 December 1917.

Lovers of old-fashioned dolls might like to visit the specialist shop **La Planel Dolls,** north of the Post Office.

St PIERRE du BOIS

St Peter-in-the-Wood or St Pierre du Bois – not a literal translation – is also known simply as St Peter's, which can be confused with St Peter Port. The parish church, known by the French name, dates from around 1375 with additions in the 15th cent, and has an impressively-large tower with 13 bells, the largest peal in the islands.

The interior still has its Victorian furnishings, and a seating plan of 1710 shows that men and women entered through separate doors and occupied different parts of the church, as is done today in most mosques.

Just north of the church are the **Coach House Galleries,** an exhibition of art for sale on two floors of a restored farm building, with a pottery and etching studio beside it; artists' materials are also on sale. The venture started in 1975 in the north and has had Sir Hugh Casson among its exhibitors. Open daily 1100-1700, may be closed Jan.

The little Quanteraine Valley has a restored waterwheel which began working in 1992. Although owned by the National Trust it is tenanted and not open, but you can see it from the main road to Fort Grey.

Fort Grey. Probably the most prominent feature in the parish is Fort Grey, named from an earlier Lieutenant-Governor by the incumbent Sir John Doyle when it was built in 1804 as protection against a French attack: its age makes it a genuine Martello tower. It replaced the 17th-cent Château de Rocquaine – 'castle on the rocky ledge' – allegedly used by the witches who also claimed Le Catioroc to the north.

The British manned Fort Grey in the First World War, the Germans in the Second, but in 1976 it became the **Maritime Museum** in a perfect setting; it's open daily Apr-Oct 1030-1230, 1330-1730, accessible by a causeway that never floods.

The museum emphasises the many ships that have been wrecked along this coast and on the Hanois Reef, where the earliest recorded loss was in 1309. Fort Grey recalls several tragedies in detail, notably the *Boreas,* a 28-gun 533-ton frigate built in Great Yarmouth in 1806 and lost on the Hanois the next year with 195 men, including its commander, Vice-Admiral Sir James Saumarez. One of *Boreas*'s cannons is on the battlements, pointing to the reef.

Copper Craft. Opposite the causeway to Fort Grey is Guernsey Copper Craft, where brass and copper utensils are made by hand in the traditional style, especially the little can peculiar to the island. You can buy a wide range of copper goods – or merely call in for cream cakes and coffee. Open daily Easter-Oct; Thur-Sun Nov-Dec.

North of Fort Grey, the Brock Battery was an extra precaution against Napoleon's attack but Fort Saumarez, whose ruins are on L'Erée peninsula, was for an earlier French threat. Several far older stones may attract your attention in this region, notably Rocque Poisson, 'Fish Rock,' on the shoreline north of Brock Battery, and La Longue Rocque near the site of the West Show. And then there's the Creux ès Faies by the car park for those planning to walk across to Lihou.

LIHOU

Lihou is the smallest permanently-inhabited of the Channel Islands, its high-tide area being 18 acres (7ha; 0.028sq miles); at low water it's part of the mainland. Access is on foot across the causeway, preferably around full or new moon when the tidal range is 30ft (9m). At first and last quarter of the moon's phases the range is just 8ft (2.5m) and Lihou remains an island for a few days.

Visitors are welcome, without dogs, but they *must obey notices about the tides* as the flood surges across the causeway with great force. The collection of dolls' houses went to Sausmarez Manor in 1992, but there's still the island itself to explore.

The first recorded visitors were monks from Mont St Michel in 1114, but they found evidence of earlier habitants in the dolmens and standing stones, which they used in building their **Priory of Nôtre Dame de la Roche.** In 1304 a priory servant murdered a monk, and was killed while being arrested by the Bailiff's men; then in 1415 Henry V seized all religious houses belonging to French orders. Lihou passed from the abbot of Mont St Michel to Eton College, which held it until the Reformation. The last known appointment of a prior was in 1560, and a century later the building was in ruins. Little remains of it today as the Germans used Lihou for target practise, but when a human skeleton was found on the island in 1962, people wondered if it could have been that of the servant, killed 658 years earlier.

A non-secular building had existed on the island for generations, replaced early this century by a proper house whose lessee – Lihou is Crown property – began drying *vraic* (seaweed) in 1926 to extract iodine. His business collapsed when foreign suppliers undercut the price. After World War Two and the rebuilding of the house, Colonel Patrick Wootton introduced Orkney sheep that thrived on seaweed, but the animals began swimming to the mainland to raid gardens. He also began summer camps for young people, and introduced Lihou's own postage stamps until the States abolished them along with the Herm stamps.

The word *lihou* is Celtic for 'mud,' and is also a common surname on Guernsey.

St SAVIOUR

St Saviour's short coast centres on Perelle Bay, a good stretch of sand with large platforms of rock exposed at low tide. To the west is Le Trépied dolmen and to the right the ruins of Fort Richmond, with **La Longue Pierre,** also known as *La Pierre de L'Essart* and *The Witch's Finger,* standing 10ft (3m) tall, the second-tallest of Guernsey's menhirs. A little way inland is another antiquity, the **Chapel of St Apolline,** the oldest building in Europe dedicated to this saint whom the Romans burned alive in Alexandria in 249. They first smashed her teeth, which is why she is now the patron saint of dentists.

A charter from Richard II, dated 1394, mentions the chapel which was then two years old. Now standing on the edge of Grande Rue, Perelle, the chapel became States property in 1873 and was restored in 1978, retaining the early frescos of the Last Supper in its single room, 27ft 2in by 13ft (8.3m by 4m). Open daily Apr-Sep 0900-2000, Oct-Mar 0900-1500.

Early morning at St Peter Port, with Herm and Jethou in the distance.

Tropical Gardens. For something completely different, try the Tropical Vinery and Gardens nearby, where pineapples, bananas, coffee, tea, rice, cotton, hibiscus, bougainvillea and citrus fruits grow in four glasshouses that once had only tomatoes. Open daily 1000-1700.

Grande Rue puts you in the right direction for the island's **reservoir,** finished in 1947 and holding up to 240,000,000 gallons (900,000cu m). Look for a car park off Rue à l'Or, from where you can walk across the dam. Guernsey's fresh water supply is seldom under stress but in times of drought you may see flooded buildings emerge.

Neuf Chemin, 'New Road,' leads south to the three-acre **Guernsey Herb Garden** at the Auberge du Val, where you can appreciate herbs for their use in the kitchen, in medicine, and simply in the garden. Open Apr-Oct 1000-1700.

Church. You are now almost at the church of St Sauveur, the largest outside of town, the weathervane on the lead-coated spire being 103ft (31m) above ground. The church was built on the site of a menhir (the Breton word means 'long stone'), the oldest surviving work being 12th cent although most is 14th and 15th cent. The tower was rebuilt in the 17th cent probably to repair lightning damage – and the 18th cent vestry was built to hold the parish artillery. The oldest gravestone in the cemetery records the death in 1602 of Nicholas Torode, but it's upside-down and left to right.

St Saviour's Tunnel. Now go *under* the church to see yet another gruesome reminder of the German Occupation. Russian and other European slave labourers carved St Saviour's Tunnel while others toiled on the near-identical shafts of the Underground Hospital. This shaft is nowhere near as large and is not as awesome, yet it has a more authentic atmosphere in its damp and dirt.

The tunnel, 18ft (5.5m) high, was to be a munitions store but was never dug to its planned extent. The British Army used it as a dump for German supplies which were accumulating across the island in massive proportions – then they sealed it.

In 1969 the seal was broken, revealing a mass of equipment rusting and rotting under 24 years' of constantly dripping water. The better stuff was sent to the Occupation Museum for restoration, while most of the remainder was left as it was – and as it now is. Open daily Apr-mid Sep, 1000-1800.

Strawberry Farm and Woodcarvers. Wander briefly south-east to the Hanging Strawberry Farm at Les Issues Vinery. Most glasshouse complexes are called 'vineries' because grapes were the island's original crop, giving way to tomatoes after London health experts expounded the love-apple's benefits. Les Issues switched from tomatoes to strawberries in 1971, growing them in heated glasshouses for fruiting nine months of the year – until the 1976 oil crisis. Now the three houses are unheated and the fruit, mostly Red Gauntlet, crops from May to October on 27,000 plants, hanging in plastic bags. You can walk around the houses, and finish with a strawberry-and-cream tea.

There's also an aviary called Nature Wonderland, amusements for the children and, on the same site, John and Janet Le Mesurier's **Guernsey Woodcarvers,** which produces and sells a wide range of carvings from a kitchen dresser to a key fob.

The Strawberry Farm is open Apr-Oct, but other attractions and the Woodcarvers are open year-round.

Gold- and Silversmiths. To the south, almost on the edge of the airport, Bruce Russell's Gold- and Silversmiths produces quality work in these precious metals; come at 1045 for a demonstration and a tour of the premises. Russell went into business in 1975, and the States commissioned him to make the island's gift for Prince Charles and Lady Diana Spencer's wedding in 1981, a silver punch bowl. Russell registered is own assay mark in 1977.

Sharing the same car park are **Sugar and Spice,** a tea-room, and **Yarn Barn** knitwear. All open year-round 0900-1700; smiths closed Sun.

CASTEL

The largest of Guernsey's parishes, Castel – or Câtel in its old French form – takes its name from the **Château du Grand Sarrasin** or Sarazin, a Viking defence which is believed to have stood on the site now occupied by the church. Guernsey folk confused Viking with 'Saracen,' another name for a Mohammedan fighting at the Crusades, because both were cruel.

Ancient man was certainly here, possibly building a burial chamber on this hillock and certainly having a menhir on the spot. The early Christians took over the pagan site and the menhir was lost until its discovery in 1878, buried under the chancel floor. This 6ft 6in (2m) tall granite goddess, probably Neolithic and around 3,000 years old, now stands in the cemetery. Nearby are some flat slabs on which the Fief St Michel held feudal court until the late 19th cent.

Church. The church of Ste Marie du Câtel, more recently called Our Lady of Deliverance, was mentioned in a Papal document of 1155, but the oldest surviving part, the western half of the north aisle, was built just a few years later. The north chancel has 13th-cent frescos and a hagioscope (a slanting slit, in this case through a pillar supporting the tower, to give a view of the altar). A sealed-up priest's door and a genuine hole in the wall – probably a cupboard where the altar vessels were kept – add to the church's mystique.

The church is almost on the parish boundary, but folklore blames this on the fairies who resented the original choice of site beside today's Les Eturs Rd in the parish centre; the little folk scattered the stones every night. As a result, Castel had medieval chapels to serve outlying districts: St Anne's at King's Mills, **St George's** on Route Delisles, St Germain's to the north, and the Victorian St Matthew's Church near Cobo. St George's chapel went in the 18th cent but nearby, on the estate of the same name, sometimes open to the public, is the feudal court-house of the Fief Le Comte and the Holy Well of St George, believed to have healing properties as legend claims St George and St Patrick met here. Legend ignores the fact that George was killed in Turkey in 303, and Patrick was born in Scotland around 387.

Vazon Bay. Castel's coast holds Vazon Bay, probably the largest stretch of sand on the island, and occasionally used for motor-cycle races in summer. Storms occasionally move enough sand to reveal the stumps of an ancient drowned forest, and if you study the sea wall at Vazon Road you will notice that the land is below high tide. This was earlier a large peat bog – *vazon* is Norman French for 'marsh' – which extended erratically to La Braye du Valle, the marshy creek which cut off northern Guernsey at high tide. **Fort Hommet**, on a headland between Vazon and Cobo bays, is one of the three genuine Martello towers, built at the same time as those in England and much desecrated between 1940 and '45.

King's Mills is the home of the **Tomato Centre and Museum,** an example of how to make a profit from growing tomatoes when most

Dusk falls in Smith St, St Peter Port.

other growers have quit. The centre gives the story of the love apple's rise in popularity and its effect on the Guernsey economy, but you can also see orchids and pearls, a cartoon cinema, and sample some tomato wine at the barbecue restaurant. Open daily Apr-Oct 1000-2100

King's Mills leads into the **Talbot Valley,** probably the most rural scene you can still find in Guernsey – and with a stream running beside the road. Several watermills operated in this vale, beginning with *Le Moulin de Bas,* then *Le Moulin du Milieu* and on to *Le Moulin de Haut,* the latter two now the names of roads though the names meant 'lower,' 'middle' and 'upper mill.' The only survivor is another mill altogether, at **Les Niaux** on the boundary with St Andrew. The large overshot waterwheel is worth seeing.

Castel's remaining attractions lie north of the church, the first being **Le Friquet Flower and Butterfly Centre,** a working nursery producing pot plants and cut bloom in 2 acres of glasshouses. The focus of interest is the butterfly house where exotic and European *lepidoptera* up to 6in (15cm) fly freely among the human visitors – but the bird-eating spiders are in glass cages. These days all attractions have to cater for wider interests, so there is a playground, mini-golf course, radio-controlled boats, and a restaurant. Open daily Easter-Oct 1000-1700.

Cobo Road leads to the **Telephone Museum** which opened in 1976 in the original Castel manual exchange, a tiny building on the east of Cobo Rd south of the one-way system, and with a car park at the rear – or you could walk from the Folk Museum. The Telephone Museum has a range of exhibits from the start of Guernsey's phone service on 28 July 1898 to the fairly recent, but its hours are limited to Apr-Sep Tues-Wed, 1900-2100.

Folk Museum. And then you reach Saumarez Park, without the 'S,' The house, built in the 18th cent by William le Marchant, came to the family de Saumarez by marriage and was the home of Admiral Sir James de Saumarez, Nelson's second-in-command during the Napoleonic Wars. Early in the 20th cent, the house became the residence of the Lieutenant-Governor as the island had no official Government House. The fourth Baron de Saumarez, retired from diplomatic service, hosted Edward, Prince of Wales, in the house in 1935. The baron died in 1937; the States bought the Park in 1938, and it became the States Offices during the war; it is now a retirement home.

The Guernsey Folk Museum, founded in 1968 and run by the National Trust of Guernsey and *La Société Guernesiaise,* is in the former stables, with its collection of agricultural machinery overflowing into the courtyard. Within the theme of preserving the island's past, the museum has re-created several aspects of farming life of a century ago when almost everybody lived off the land or the sea.

Grandma and grandpa lived in their little stone-built thatched cottage, providing by their own labour as much of their food and clothing as possible. The first tourists were arriving from England, travelling the island in horse-carts, and as a result, English was beginning to replace the *patois* so that a half-tester bed became, ungrammatically, 'un victoria,' and replaced the *lit de fouaille* or 'bed of fern.'

The Victorian Bedroom shows the farmer's wife with her new baby; the Kitchen has a woman taking bread from the oven and a table set for dinner; upstairs, for modern convenience, is *la Grande Tchérue*, the Great Plough, 41ft (12.5m) long. It dwarfs the display of fishing gear. The dairy and wash-house outside use much wood, brass and copper, and the cider barn has a horse-powered apple-crusher made in 1734: note its elaborate wooden screw. Open daily Easter-Oct, 1000-1730.

Battle of Flowers. Jersey's Battle of Flowers began in 1902 and is one of the major events of the Channel Islands' summer season, but since 1930 Guernsey has had its own battle, held as part of the North Agricultural Show, in the grounds of Saumarez Park in late August.

Preparing for the annual rowing race from Dixcart Bay, Sark, to St Catherine's Bay, Jersey.

VALE

The northern parishes of Vale and St Sampson are both split in two, their main common boundary running along the route of the Braye du Valle that was flooded at each high tide, making northern Vale an island. Lt-Gen Sir John Doyle, who drained the marsh, also built the *Route Militaire* across the reclaimed land.

Church. The western part of Vale has some small bays with moderate beaches, but no other attraction for the visitor – so let's start with the church St Michel du Valle built on a small hill on the northern edge of that former inlet; there's even a ring in the church wall for people to moor their boats. Monks from Mont St Michel built a priory here around 968; it was consecrated in 1117, but the oldest surviving structures are the chancel and parts of the choir, the latter originally the monks' quarters, both dating from around 1155, the year when a Papal document listed the priory among its assets. In the later building, the nave and chancel are not in a straight line, no two walls are parallel, and no corner is a perfect 90° angle.

A French Protestant priest was appointed in 1585 and the parish stayed Calvinist until an Anglican took the living in 1662 – but most services were in French until 1920, and the church records until 1939.

Vale Castle. The castle at Vale commands a good view of shore and sea from atop its hillock, but the best view of it is from the road; its bailey (wall) is all there is to see. The original was probably 12th cent on an Iron Age site, but the oldest surviving structure is early 15th cent. Barracks, added in the late 18th cent, were occupied by Russian troops who had served in the Netherlands in 1799 and 1800; the many who died of disease picked up in the Dutch wetlands are buried just outside the castle gate. Early in the 20th cent those same barracks were home to quarrymen and their families, but the occupying Germans demolished them, one of their few good deeds on the island. The castle is never closed.

The road north passes the high-tide fishing-harbour at Bordeaux – the name means 'beside the waters' – and soon there's low-tide access across the sands to the Guernsey National Trust island of **Hommet Paradis,** mentioned in Hugo's *Toilers of the Sea*.

Les Marais Road leads west to the **Koi Farm,** for a splendid display of these fish as well as a collection of cacti, open daily 0900-1700. But if you go north you'll find the Déhus dolmen and, a few bends later, the **Beaucette Marina,** also known as the Channel Island Yacht Marina, a sheltered anchorage for luxury yachts in an old quarry. North again is Fort Doyle, built by that busy Lt-Governor but desecrated by its German occupants.

The open grassland of L'Ancresse Common, popular with golfers and rabbits, has six pseudo-Martello towers protecting it from invasion; Duke Robert of Normandy, on his way to help Alfred the

Great fight Canute, is claimed to have used L'Ancresse Bay as an anchorage – which is how it got its name.

La Varde Dolmen. Near the 17th green on the golf course La Varde Dolmen stands prominent: it should, as it's the largest in Guernsey with a main chamber 36ft (11m) long by 13ft (4m) at its widest, and with one of its capstones 16ft (5m) long: how could early man move such objects? There's a smaller Stone Age tomb, *L'Autel des Landes,* by the 6th green, and by the 5th green is **Les Fouaillages,** a cluster of small burial chambers whose main interest is the pottery some 6,500 years old, discovered here after the excavation of 1978. And so we find ourselves back at Vale Church.

St SAMPSON

There's a macabre sense of humour in the gravestone in St Sampson's church which explains that Thomas Falla was killed in 1799 by a 26lb (11kg) cannonball 'lodged between the main and secondary bones of his thigh.' This is Guernsey's oldest parish church, standing near the spot where St Sampson landed around 550 on his mission to preach in the island; he had studied in Wales under St Illtud, with Branwalader (who may have become the St Brelade who settled in Jersey) as fellow-disciple.

The oldest parts of the church are the nave and chancel, which were completed by 1350, giving St Sampson's the most rudimentary tower, with a saddleback (double-pitched) roof. It stood on the shores of the Braye du Valle, diagonally opposite Vale Church.

Where the horse-carriages ply for business on Sark, with the NatWest Bank in the background.

St Sampson's Harbour. The harbour at St Sampson was an extension of the flooded inlet, and part of the quay at the harbour's head is still known as Bridge St, marking the crossing-point. In the 18th cent, around 300 ships were built here and along the coast to the south, the death of the trade matching the growth in the export of granite in the new iron-hulled ships.

In the 19th cent John Loudon Macadam experimented with roadbuilding in Ayrshire and Cornwall, and concluded that finely-crushed stone mixed with tar – 'tarmacadam' – should form the top layer. Guernsey granite was ideal, and exports rose from 12,000 tons annually to 450,000 in 50 years. The 20th-cent development of asphalt, which uses limestone, killed the trade, and now St Sampson's Harbour repairs small vessels and does some horticultural export business.

Château des Marais. Almost on the boundary with St Peter Port, the Château des Marais, 'Castle of the Marshes' or just Ivy Castle, is a ruin standing on a hillock amid what was once marshland. Access now is through the drab Grand Bouet Estate of public housing looking more decrepit than the castle, which was begun soon after King John lost his French territories. It was in ruins in the 16th cent and what you see today are the partial repairs of the 18th cent against another French threat. Within earshot, but not accessible from here, is the island's **karting** track.

St Sampson's tourist attractions are in the middle of the parish. **Guernsey Candles** offers one of the best collections of candles you're likely to see, and they're far too good to light. Some are moulded in coloured wax, producing glossy or matt works that could be confused with marble or poreclain until you touch them, while others are carved and curved with special knives while the wax is still warm. Open daily 0900-1730; ~2130 May-Sep.

The nearby **Oatlands Craft Centre,** set on a seven-acre (3ha) site which was a major brickworks, gives you the opportunity to see delicate glassware being blown and pots being turned on a wheel. Part of the brickworks, which are listed as ancient monuments, hold a museum to the humble brick, but if you'd rather peer into an active beehive, here's your chance. The potters and glassblowers established the centre and invited the other craftspersons to join them, so now you have a cosmetics workshop, a small-animal farm, a silversmith, a glass engraver – and the ubiquitous restaurant and play area for the children. Open daily 1000-1730, closed Sun Oct-Apr.

Guernsey craftsmen of whatever skill have come a very long way since mass-production gave charisma to their work, and mass-tourism made them available to us all.

9: ALDERNEY

The fortified island

ALDERNEY IS THE MOST HEAVILY FORTIFIED of the Channel Islands because, at 8.3 miles (13.5km), it is the closest to France. It was the only island to be near-totally evacuated during World War Two and as a result it had the only German death camp on British soil. It was the very last territory in Europe to be liberated after the German surrender; and it is the most northerly of the group, which made it the first British possession to see the Spanish Armada in 1588. It escaped feudalism by being owned by the Bishop of Coutances, yet its poor land was farmed in the medieval strip system until early this century.

Wide open. Alderney looks to the sea more than does any other Channel island and, with few hedges and trees, its windswept and open interior seldom lacks a sea view in at least one direction. Jersey has its deep, wooded valleys, Guernsey its introspective country lanes, Sark its tree-lined hedgerows, but Alderney is open – open to the wind and the rain, and to the threat of invasion. Yet, conversely, this openness gives a sense of freedom, a lack of claustrophobia that the other islands experience.

It's the closest to Britain yet it has fewer visitors than the other islands, with almost all Britons coming by air to land at the Channel Islands' first airport, opened in 1935, which is now one of the smallest international airports in the world with two of its runways still grass. At one time it had the world's only female airport controller, Miss W. le Cocq. French visitors? They fly in from Cherbourg or Dinard or come by boat.

For much of its history Alderney has needed to be aware of what was happening on the mainland, territory which has usually been hostile. This caution explains the Telegraph Tower, built in 1811 in the south-west, almost on the island's highest ground and able to communicate with St Peter Port and Sark; it explains the forts, begun in 1546 but completed by the Victorians; it explains the vast breakwater, begun in 1847; and *that* explains the quarries and the Channel Islands' first, and only surviving, railway.

Ancient visitors. Alderney has been open to visitors since the dawn of history. About 2,000 Bronze Age tools have been found on

Longis (Longy) Common, most on the site of the so-called 'old town,' which folklore claims was buried by drifting sand. Neolithic inhabitants left a midden nearby, and Iron Age inhabitants made pots on a site now 300ft (100m) west of where the Romans built their fort, *Castrum Longini*. Then in 1546 Henry VIII ordered the building of the Chateau de Longis, also known as *Les Murs de Bas,* the 'Lower Walls,' on the site of the Roman castle, which wasn't totally lost. In later generations the building came to be known as **The Nunnery,** probably because the troops garrisoned there found it so inhospitable. It's now a private house.

Henry, by the way, had seized Boulogne in 1544 with 40,000 men, and was trying to split France, but he called it off in 1547.

Status Insulae. Duke William of Normandy loaned Alderney to the Abbot of Mont St Michel in 1042; the abbot yielded in 1057 to the Bishop of Coutances who administered the island in an unusual alliance. A document of 1236, the *Status Insulae de Aurineo* set out the rights of the monarch and the bishop, and the authority that devolved from them: a Court composed of a *Prévot* (sheriff) and six *jurats* (judges), which eventually became the island's government, the States of Alderney. It survived, with minor variations, until 1949.

The *Status Insulae,* a kind of Domesday Book, recalls that Aurineo had a windmill, owned directly by Henry III – which makes it one of the earliest recorded in northern Europe, though there's no trace of it today. The Bishop of Coutances, who owned the island's water mill, appointed all priests until 1568 when the Bishop of Winchester took

Some of Alderney's streets are quiet, even in August...

over – but Protestant king and Catholic bishop still jointly ruled for many years, and the first indoor meeting of the Alderney Court, in 1770, had representatives from both parties.

John Chamberlain bought the governorship of Alderney from the Crown, then sold it in 1591 to Robert Devereux, 2nd Earl of Essex, who sacked Cádiz in 1596 but failed to put down an Irish rebellion in 1599. Dismissed from the Royal Court he led a rebellion against Elizabeth I the next year and was executed in 1601. Despite his anti-Royalist act, the fortress of Les Murs de Haut, the 'Upper Walls,' which he bought in 1591 for £1,000, was renamed **Essex Castle** in his honour. Essex, who never lived on the island, leased his governorship to John Chamberlain's brother William, whose family held it until 1643.

John Le Mesurier. Guernseyman John Le Mesurier – pronounced *mezz-oo-ree-eh* – inherited the governorship from the Chamberlains via the Carterets and the Andros family. In 1736 his son Henry built the small jetty which survives at Braye, so replacing the difficult harbour in Longis Bay. Henry's brother, another John Le Mesurier, succeeding him, built Government House, now the **Island Hall** and Library. Governor Peter Le Mesurier built **Les Mouriaux House,** Alderney's smartest home, which became the President's residence and is now private. Another John Le Mesurier followed with the town school in 1790; it's now the **Museum,** open Wed-Mon 1000-1200, Tues 1400-1600 for £1. It was this John, the last hereditary governor, who made a vast fortune from privateering activities, in one year earning almost £135,000. And his son, the Rev John Le Mesurier, used some of the proceeds to pay for St Anne's Church, consecrated by the Bishop of Winchester in 1850.

The forts. Back in 1739 the island Court, always aware of big brother France on the skyline, had urged the building of defences at nine vulnerable places on the coast and, beginning in 1845, they were greatly improved in preparation for an attack from a France which was seething with unrest; Cherbourg harbour had been strengthened, with a breakwater large enough to shelter the entire fleet, but the unrest erupted in 1848 into the Second Revolution which saw Louis Philippe deposed.

The largest was **Fort Albert,** east of Braye Bay, the most important of the 13 and the only one to be garrisonned regularly, its capacity being 2,000 troops. Today it's empty. Going clockwise, **Château à l'Etoc,** 'Stack Castle,' on the northernmost headland, has been converted into apartments. **Fort Corblets** ('cor–blay') had six guns in 1886 but is now a private house. **Fort les Homeaux Florains,** ('ommoh flor-an') on a high-tide isle accessible by a causeway, is in ruins, but it was here that the four-masted sailing ship *Liverpool* was wrecked in February 1902; **Fort Houmet Herbé** ('oo-may err-bay') on another islet, used to have 68-pound guns but is also ruined.

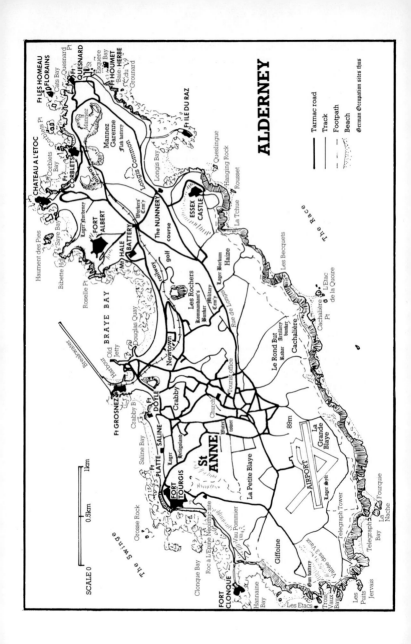

ALDERNEY

Tarmac road
Track
Footpath
Beach
German Occupation sites thus

SCALE 0   0.5km   1km

Fort Ile du Raz ('eel doo razz') overlooks Longis Bay, the earlier harbour, and is in good repair: cricket commentator John Arlott, who retired to Alderney in 1981, wanted to buy it and for a while it was a restaurant before becoming a **Bird Museum**. The **Château de Longis,** ('longy') 'The Nunnery,' was not strengthened.

Essex Castle, the old 'Murs du Haut,' was equipped as a military hospital shortly after it was built, but was never used as such. There's a long stretch of unfortified cliff along the south coast, the next defence being **Fort Clonque** ('klonk') on its little isle, accessible by a causeway and part converted into holiday homes. **Fort Tourgis,** ('tor-zhee') empty and decaying, was a large barrack block. The small shoreline battery of **Fort Platte Saline** ('plat sal-een') is now the base for a company which exports an endless supply of sand from Saline Bay. Little **Fort Doyle** shared the guarding of Crabby Bay with **Fort Grosnez,** 'big nose,' ('gro-nay') which also controlled the breakwater; today it houses staff and equipment who maintain that massive sea defence.

All the forts not in private ownership belong to the States of Alderney which bought them from the British Government for a small sum. They are **not open** to the public.

The Breakwater. Cherbourg had its giant breakwater in 1842. So the British Government, almost in a panic, decided that Portland Bill in Dorset, and Alderney, must each have one – but the officials never asked Alderney fishermen, who knew the winter storms and would have advised against the project. In 1847 work began on Portland and on Alderney; on the latter, a railway had to be built to carry the thousands of tons of stone to be quarried from the east of the island. Irish labourers escaped their famine by coming here, and a regular sea link from Guernsey brought food and other materials. The mole was finished in 1864 at a cost of £1,500,000, far beyond budget, its curved tip stretching 4,827ft (1,471m) across Braye Bay – and it suffered two large breaches within the year. Soon it was obvious that nothing could save the seaward end, so 1,780ft (542m) were abandoned, and continue to be a hazard to shipping.

In 1872 an inquiry in London, hearing a deputation from Alderney, agreed that as Britain had built the thing for its own use, Britain should maintain it. And so it did, until the Falklands War, when the States of Jersey gave £5,000,000 and the States of Guernsey gave £100,000 to the Falklands Fund, both sympathising with islanders suffering occupation in time of war. Westminster demanded a contribution to the military cost in addition, stating the UK would do for the Channel Islands what it did for the Falklands but forgetting that in 1925 it decided the islands were undefendable. Jersey concurred, but Guernsey refused, agreeing to take over the maintenance of Alderney breakwater instead. The news was a major blow to

Alderney folk hoping to restore total independence, but everybody agrees that the mole has helped defend Braye Beach from erosion.

War. The island saw terrible crimes against humanity during the war, according to claims that Solomon Steckoll makes in his book *The Alderney Death Camp*. It is beyond dispute that there were four *Konzentrationslager*, concentration camps: Lager Nordeney overlooking Saye Bay, east of Fort Albert; Lager Heligoland east of Fort Tourgis; Lager Borkum south of Longis House on Longis Road; and the worst of them all, Lager Sylt, on the edge of the airfield.

It is also beyond dispute that hundreds of prisoners were murdered, by strangulation, shooting, hanging, or beating, and that hundreds more died of starvation and exposure, the total probably around 4,000, with 3,000 of them being Russians. British troops who liberated the island quickly found several hundred bodies buried on Longis Common, some in mass graves. But there is almost no trace left of any of the camps, nor of most of the other German buildings, exceptions being the anti-tank walls in Longy and Saline bays, a water tower, and some gun emplacements.

The horror perpetrated on the island was so intense that the land birds fled, as they did from the concentration camps in Poland. They came back to Alderney in 1950.

When the human inhabitants returned in November 1945 they found many houses destroyed, the economy shattered, and the fields neglected – the *Wehrmacht* had failed in its attempt to turn Alderney

...but it's difficult to find parking space in Victoria St, St Anne.

into a granary isle. Options offered were to abandon the island, to merge it with Hampshire, or with Guernsey. The islanders reluctantly chose to subject themselves to Guernsey, so losing an independence that had endured for centuries. Hitler's legacy is that the States of Alderney is now little more than a town council.

AROUND ALDERNEY

As your Trislander aircraft comes in to land at the tiny airport you may notice the turbulence on the sea south of Alderney. This is **The Race,** one of the strongest currents in Europe, which has been recorded at 11 knots (12.5mph, 20kph) at spring tide off the Brinchetais Ledge by Houmet Herbé, and 12kts (13.8mph, 22kph) off Cap de la Hague; this is a good speed for an ordinary cyclist. **The Swinge,** between Alderney and Burhou, also visible from your plane, reaches 9kts in the middle of a spring tide.

There's a taxi stand outside the airport but you may have to use the public phone to call a cab. No problem; it's only a 10-minute walk to St Anne, which will allow you to ponder why, after the trauma of the Occupation, the house called *Pasadena* has a German letter-box.

St Anne. St Anne is a pleasant town, some of its cobbled streets so quiet, even in August, that you may think everybody has fled the island again. Marais Square, the heart of the original *Ville*, has a few cars parked where, earlier this century, weekly cattle markets were held; before that, women washed their linen in the stream that ran through *Le Marais*, which is French for 'swamp.' The island's first courts were held in Le Huret, the street which leads to Connaught Square – St Anne's Sq before the Duke of Connaught visited in 1905 – and the original Government House, now the Island Hall. The German Kommandant's HQ was on the square's west side. West, Les Mouriaux street has Mouriaux House, the home of Le Mesuriers, not open to the public, and **Alderney Pottery** which welcomes visitors: watch pots being thrown, then have a light meal.

East, Le Huret passes the former school, now the **Museum,** which has a good collection of Iron Age relics from the site west of The Nunnery on Longis Common as well as mementos of World War Two. Its neighbour, the clock tower, is all that remains of the original church.

Now Le Huret becomes High St, leading out to Longis Rd, but a left turn takes you into Victoria St, the commercial heart of the town. If you thought everybody had gone, think again: they're probably looking for a parking place in Victoria St, which was Rue Grosnez until Queen Victoria paid the island its first royal visit. The street was built when St Anne expanded to accommodate the men working on the forts.

The **Tourist Office** is opposite the entry into Queen Elizabeth II St, known as **QE II St,** but which was New St until the Queen's visit in 1957;

Douglas Quay gave Alderney a tiny harbour long before the breakwater was built.

it began life as Rue des Héritiers. Here is the **States Office,** the Police and the small jail, and the **Court House.** To complicate matters, the States meets in the Court House, built in 1850, gutted during the Occupation, and reopened in 1955 when the Jurats wore their traditional robes for the first time in 15 years. The assembly chamber, which has a painting of the last Governor John Le Mesurier surrendering his title to the Crown in 1825, is open to visitors who ask at the office downstairs. The police force has three constables and a sergeant, all loaned from the Guernsey force; special constable and unofficial traffic warden George Partridge retired in 1993 in his late 60s.

Midway down Victoria St is **St Anne's Church,** the work of Rev John Le Mesurier. The *Wehrmacht* desecrated the building, used it as a wine cellar, dumped the altar in a field, pushed over the gravestones, mounted machine guns in the tower – German soldiers' names are still carved in the masonry there – and stole the bells. They were found in a field near Cherbourg, re-tuned in Loughborough, and re-hung in 1953.

Beyond the **Post Office** (Mon-Sat 0830-1230, plus 1330-1700 *not* Wed, Sat), Victoria St ends, the road left leading out of town to the golden sands of Saline Bay and the grey sands of Crabby Bay. The road ahead leads to the cricket ground and village green, known as the **Butes** from the days when archers trained at their butts here. To the right is Braye Rd, leading down to the harbour.

Alderney's **Harbour** is picturesque if you look in the correct direction, with a ramp leading down to the splendid sands of Braye Bay and the old Douglas Quay, now seldom used. Braye Street is lined with 18th-cent houses on one side and Victorian warehouses on the other, and the bollards you see are cannon probably from HMS *Amethyst*, wrecked in The Swinge in 1796. There's a good view of the island from the breakwater, but *don't risk the walk in a westerly wind at high tide.*

Railway. Braye Road Station is where you board the only train still operating in the Channel Islands. The Germans ripped up the track and sent it to Cherbourg for scrap, replacing it with metre-gauge to link with their 60cm-track in their quarries. After the war the 4ft 8½in gauge was relaid, but quarrying never resumed, leaving the line idle for years.

In 1978 the new Alderney Railway Society revived the services, using diesel loco D100, no 2271, built at Newton-le-Willows in 1949, then from 1982 steam loco J.T.DALY, 'number 3.' Rolling stock is either open wagons with simple roofs, or coaches rescued from the London Underground. Trains leave Braye Sat, Sun, Bank hols, and Wed in summer, 1400, 1500, 1600, for a 45-minute round trip to Mannez Quarry in the far east. It's not an exotic destination, but it's where the breakwater rock came from. Mannez is pronounced *Moh-nay*, which describes the foghorn at nearby **Mannez Lighthouse,** open to the public on clear afternoons.

Seeing Alderney. If you're here for a day, I recommend you walk from the airport and explore St Anne on foot; another walk can take you from Braye to Mannez and back along Rue de Longis to the airport. Or you can hire a cycle to make it easier. Or take a bus ride from the terminus in Marais Square; the route is similar to the suggested walk.

If you're here for longer, there's time to take the **coastal path,** possibly making two days of it. You'll need a good map as there is no continuous route, but this will give you the chance to explore the rugged south coast. You could take the path down to the tiny **Cachalière Pier** from where rock was shipped; you might find the 65ft-long (20m) tunnel from Lager Sylt to the Kommandant's chalet. You might also go down to the beach at **Telegraph Bay,** a good yacht anchorage on an ebb (west-flowing) tide, but don't swim far out as the ebb has a powerful inshore current – and don't be so engrossed in the magnificent caves that you are caught by the rising tide.

The cliffs at Alderney's western tip are gashed by the steep-sided **Vallée de Trois Vaux,** the Valley of Three Streams; access to the shingly beach is difficult, and the climb back up to the plateau is steep, but it's a picturesque spot.

Your walk will also show you most of the island's arable land,

Braye Bay has a splendid, sheltered beach on Alderney's northern coast.

seldom cultivated as the soil is too poor. In the 1950s and '60s Alderney exported carrots to Britain, but now it grows little more than a field or two of cereals on La Petite Blaye and, since 1992, it imports its fruit and vegetables from France aboard the *Trondenes* car ferry.

BURHOU

North-west of Alderney sits Burhou, a flattish isle no more than 70ft (21m) above high tide and 3,200ft (1.1km) long. It almost quadruples its size at low tide, and includes for a few hours, Little Burhou, which has altitude of 43ft (13m). The only building is a reconstructed stone hut for dedicated birdwatchers, who must seek permission from the States Office in QE II St to stay overnight – but not between 1 April and mid-July, the nesting season for the gannets, puffins, gulls and petrels who call this home. German gunners on the Giffoine hillock, Alderney, used the original stone hut for target practice and undoubtedly killed a number of birds as well, although there's no record of their shooting at the **Garden Rocks,** Les Etacs, off Alderney's western tip, where gannets established a colony in 1940. They were the only inhabitants not to be affected by the Occupation.

10: SARK

Feudalism lives on

SARK IS UNIQUE in many respects. It is the world's smallest self-governing country, based on population (if it *is* a country, and that's arguable); it has what is claimed to be the world's smallest harbour (also arguable); it is the only self-contained community in Europe to ban the motor car; and it is the only country in the world where an immigrant may get a seat in the Government as soon as he buys a property – but that immigrant *must be a British citizen.* Along with Andorra it is the last stronghold of feudalism in Europe; and the island bans all aircraft overflights lower than 500ft unless it be a helicopter on a mercy mission.

Sark is also starkly different from the other Channel Islands. Many of its homes and shops are built of concrete blocks and roofed with corrugated iron sheet, and although it is small – 1,348 acres, 2.1 sq miles, 544ha – few properties have a sea view. Why not? Because its original settlers who came with Helier de Carteret in 1565 or who were already here, hid their homes from storms and passing ships, although they kept a lookout for unwelcome visitors.

Arrival. You reach Sark by sea, either from Jersey or Guernsey, almost always disembarking at **Maseline Harbour,** rebuilt in 1949, and then walking through a tunnel carved in 1866. The other option, more likely if you're in your own boat, is to use tiny **Creux Harbour** just to the south, whose breakwater was built in 1588 by de Carteret's son although the tunnel dates from 1563.

Other landing places are perilous except in calm seas: L'Eperquerie in the north, where Helier de Carteret first set foot, which gives access to **L'Eperquerie Common,** the former *Pècherie* where fish were dried; Banquette; Rouge Terrier and the sheltered Port Gorey on Little Sark, the latter once used for exporting silver ore; Havre Gosselin on the west coast, where a jetty was built in 1912; Port du Moulin near the Seigneurie; and two landings on Brechou itself. Depending on the wind, yachts can anchor in Grand Grève, west of La Coupée, and in Dixcart Bay, (pronounced *dee-car*); come to Sark for the start of the **boat race** to Jersey and you'll see Dixcart Bay crowded.

Harbour Hill. From Creux or Maseline, Harbour Hill presents a steep 300ft (100m) climb, which you can take either by tractor-trailer for 40p, or on foot – try the narrow path alongside the main road and you may see some of the island's enormous wild rhubarb.

If you're staying in any of the island hotels except the Aval du Creux, your luggage will go ahead by tractor, but you may not travel with it: from the top of Harbour Hill your choice of transport is on foot, by cycle, or horse carriage. The carriages stand by the Bel Air Tavern awaiting their customers at £4 per person for a two-hour ride, which does not include Little Sark as carriages are not allowed across the causeway. Cycles are available behind the Bel Air or on The Avenue, at £2 for the day; in high summer reserve your cycle or carriage when you book your ferry. The carriage drivers are good local guides but most are young Britons on a working holiday.

AROUND SARK

The most obvious way to go is straight ahead, but if you turn right at La Collinette crossroads into Rue Lucas, the **Mermaid Tavern** is soon in view along Rue Hotton, another right turn. Continue down here and you eventually reach the **lighthouse,** built in 1912 150ft (50m) up the cliffs of Pointe Robert, and open to visitors 1300 to sunset in good weather.

Back on Rue Lucas, you pass the old telephone exchange which, until automation came in the 1980s, was the focal point of communica-

One of the charming little houses on Little Sark.

tions; people would give the telephonist a name rather than a number, and she might route the call to a shop or a neighbour's house to make the connection. The next crossroads is called just that, but in French – Le Carrefour – and if you continue straight over onto Rue du Fort you'll eventually reach La Banquette landing. But for now, turn right onto Rue Pot for the descent to the bay of **Grève de la Ville,** with its natural arch called **Chapelle des Mauves,** 'Gull Chapel,' although *mouette* is the bird's usual name. Among the many caverns is **Dog Cave,** which emits a barking sound as the tide invades it.

South from La Collinette the road plunges into the steep-sided and wooded Baker's Valley which hides the Dixcart Hotel, the island's oldest, and Stocks, almost as old. Footpaths plunge down through springtime beds of bluebells and primroses to **Dixcart Bay,** the most easily accessible of Sark's beaches, where there's a natural arch and a cave 375ft (115m) deep. Dixcart got its name from the French *dix cartes,* 'ten cards,' but nobody remembers why.

Another path leads to the **Hog's Back,** a gorse-covered peninsula, and to **Derrible Bay** and Creux Derrible, an impressive *souffleur,* a 'blowhole cave.'

The Avenue. Back at La Collinette, Sark's main street, The Avenue – known locally as the M1 – leads west. The Avenue is a revelation, with unpretentious shops usually opening straight onto the crushed-stone street, and with more than half the plots empty. The Midland and NatWest banks guard The Avenue's entrance, then you have Avenue Gifts, Studio Sark, Sark Glass, the Little Shop, Jackson's cycle hire, a jeweller, ices and yoghourt, Sark Pefumery, the Gift Shop, Mell's Restaurant, more gifts, Sark Stores and Bakery, Rendezvous Stores, and finally the Gallery Stores and post office.

From here you have another choice of road. Right, north, takes you to **St Peter's Church,** built in 1820 for £1,000, its bells cast from cannon belonging to the disbanded Sark Militia; then Dairy Mary; the Island Hall, for public meetings and entertainment; to the former boys' school, which is also Sark's government building, the home of the **Chief Pleas** at least three times a year. When the Pleas is in session the children have a day off lessons, and islanders and visitors are admitted to the proceedings.

Some years ago the Agricultural Committee of the Chief Pleas offered a bounty on the legs of magpies and carrion crows as well as on the tails of rabbits; another committee is responsible for the diesel-generator at the top of Harbour Hill; yet another controls the isle's water supply from boreholes; and another conducts driving tests on tractors and issues the driving licences valid nowhere else in the world.

The Seigneurie. Beyond the crossroads at Clos à Jaôn, Rue de la Rade leads to the Seigneurie, now the ancestral home of the Seigneur

The tower of Sark's Seigneurie rises through the treetops.

although it began as La Perronerie, the home of one of the original tenants who came here in 1565, for Helier de Carteret lived in Le Manoir. The oldest part of the warm-grey stone house dates from that year 1565, with the main part built in 1730 by Dame Suzanne Le Pelley, the first ruler of Sark to live in the house. The dominant square signalling-tower is the work of Seigneur the Rev W T Collings, who was reluctant to cut the trees that had masked the original tower that sent and received messages from Guernsey. And the Sark flag that you see has the Normandy leopards, not the English lions, *couchant* in the top left canton.

The Seigneurie is never open to the public, but its gardens are, on Wed, Fri, Bank Hols, 1000-1700, the attractions being the splendid display of flowers, including some sub-tropical specimens, the island's only dove-cote (nobody but the Seigneur is allowed to keep doves or pigeons), and a saker (a form of cannon) inscribed *Don de sa Majesté la Royne Elizabeth au Seigneur de Sercq, AD 1572 –* 'given by Her Majesty Queen Elizabeth...' The cannon came from the Tower of London and its carriage is claimed to be of wood from *HMS Victory*.

The Seigneurie is on the site of the 6th-cent **monastery of St Magliore,** and two of the monks' small chapels have survived.

Tarnished silver. In 1834 Seigneur Pierre Le Pelley became a major investor in the new Hope Mining Company, formed to exploit a silver deposit found in Little Sark. Pierre drowned in a boatwreck off Bec du Nez, Sark's northernmost tip, allowing his brother Ernest to

A muscovy duck watches the tide come in at St Peter Port.

become Seigneur. Ernest soon found that the fortune in silver was perpetually elusive, so he mortgaged his fief to **John Allaire** of Jethou for £4,000. The island's population in the 1831 census had been 543, but by 1841 it stood at 790 after an influx of miners from Cornwall.

Finally there was enough silver to warrant a shipment to England, but the captain diverted to Guernsey so he could visit his sick wife. His boat was wrecked on the larger island with the loss of all her crew and the precious cargo, and on that same day the sea broke through into a mineshaft, drowning 10 men and killing all hope for the Hope Mining Company. Seigneur Ernest Le Pelley died in 1847 and his son, Peter Carey Le Pelley, finding himself unable to repay the mortgage, sold the fief haubert of Sark to Allaire's daughter, widow Marie Collings, who became Dame of Sark four generations removed from the better-known Dame Sibyl Hathaway.

South of the Seigneurie is La Moinerie Hotel, converted from a farmhouse built in 1728, while north of it a path leads to Port du Moulin, which takes its name from an ancient watermill. On the way down, look for the **Window,** a hole cut through a rock ledge to allow 19th-cent farmers to haul *vraic* up from the beach.

Far north. Rue la Rade continues to L'Eperquerie Common and a selection of cannon rescued from the *Valentine,* wrecked off Brechou in 1781. The cliffs have a wide choice of sea caves, notably **Les Boutiques,** the second-largest complex on Sark and well worth a visit at low water on the spring tide; a tunnel leads north to emerge almost at the island's northernmost tip. The Boutiques – 'Shops' – took their name from the legend that smugglers stored their wares here, but that was a crazy idea as the first storm would have emptied the caves completely.

On the east coast of this rugged headland, Les Fontaines Bay holds two natural arches which Sark artist William Topliss called the **Fairy Grotto;** the bay's other end offers the **Creux Bélet,** a jagged slash in the cliffs, and Red Cave, optionally called Horse Cave. The path up to Le Fort, one of the original tenements, reveals a wonderfully panoramic view.

Jail. Back at the western end of The Avenue, you have the option of continuing west, by what was the girls' school before co-education arrived, and with the tiny twin-cell jail in its grounds, built in 1856. The jail can still be used if needed, either for an errant Sarkee or for a drunken tourist; the original maximum sentence was *trois fois quatre-vingt heures,* or three days, but 48 hours is now the maximum incarceration, after which the prisoner must be transferred to St Peter Port.

On the bend of the road stands Le Manoir, the home of Helier de Carteret and later seignieurs, then Rue du Moulin wanders on past the **windmill,** built in 1571 and now standing sailless and forlorn on the island's highest point, 375ft (114m). The Seigneur still has exclusive rights to the milling of Sarkese corn, but this mill has not ground for almost a century.

The Vaurocque Crossroads is ahead. Right and left leads to Petit Champ ('Small Field') Hotel; straight ahead takes you to the **Pilcher Monument** which commemorates the London merchant Jeremiah Giles Pilcher, his three companions and a boatman, who "embarked in a sailing gig from the bay below this spot at 5pm on 19 October 1868 and were all lost during a squall..." The bay in question is Havre Gosselin, once popular with fishermen.

South of Gosselin, the **Victor Hugo Cave** on Longue Pointe, named from an illustrious early visitor, is accessible only by boat; don't swim, as the currents are strong. North of Havre Gosselin the **Gouliot Caves,** Sark's largest, are accessible on foot at lowest water, when you may find sea anemones of many colours clinging to the walls.

Brechou. Around 600ft (200m) away lies Brechou or Brecqhou, earlier known as Ile de Marchands from its previous 'tenants.' Dame Sibyl Hathaway sold the island in 1929 for £3,000, and in 1949 it sold for £15,000 to Thomson and Alastair Donaldson, founders of the Donbros clothing company. They sold it in 1966 for £44,000 to industrialist Leonard Matcham, who used his seat in the Chief Pleas to get permission to land his helicopter on the island. All owners of the island have kept it as a private domain.

Sark Lark. While multi-millionaires have bought entire islands, such as Jethou and Brechou, other men of money looked at Sark's absence of Income Tax and its relaxed attitude to company law, and devised a scheme for persuading ordinary islanders to become non-executive directors of a range of companies. The islanders' fees were small, but their presence in the tax haven allowed the companies to offset taxes. The States of Guernsey strongly disapproved of the scheme as its policy is to make absolutely certain that all financial deals are above suspicion, but while the so-called Sark Lark lasted, Sarkese who had multiple directorships made a substantial income for doing virtually nothing.

Turn left at the Vaurocque Crossroads and you are heading due south towards Little Sark, passing on your right George Guille's house. George hires his boat, the *Non Pareil,* for the day – a leisurely cruise around the rugged coast is an ideal trip for anybody staying several days on the island.

La Coupée. Little Sark will be a separate island a few thousand years from now, as the sea is attacking the isthmus that joins it to the rest of Sark. Until the end of World War Two the only land access to Little Sark was across La Coupée – 'the cut' – a razorback ridge of rocks with a 250ft (80m) drop to the sea on each side; on windy days children crawled over on their way to school, and as it was impossible to carry sacks of grain, Little Sark had its own windmill. German prisoners of war built the present 10ft (3m) railed causeway and its steep access routes, which are vital to Little Sark's existence. Tractors take luggage across to La Sablonnerie, 'the sand-pit,' the only hotel, but horse carriages never use La Coupée.

Little Sark. The peninsula's attractions are its coastline and its intimacy, with tiny cottages clustered around the hotel, whose roof at one point reaches down to chest height. A path leads down past an old cider press to **The Pot,** the second-largest creux (blowhole cave) on the island. There's a derelict silver mine here, but the others are in the south, overlooking Port Gorey, with nothing more than the pithead buildings remaining. If you have young children, be particularly careful they don't fall down any shafts.

A maze of paths, not well signed, leads down to **Venus's Pool,** a low-tide bathing area around 20ft (6m) deep and, at Sark's southernmost tip, **Jupiter's Pool.** Clamber around Plat Roé Bay for the Gorey Souffleur and the less impressive Teddy Bath, another low-tide pool. On Little Sark's western tip is **Adonis's Pool,** similar to Venus's and equally exposed for around four hours at low water.

Cliff-climbing around here is exhilarating, but you must be extremely careful of slippery rocks, rogue waves (avoid the area if the seas are rough), and the incoming tide.

Beware of falling in love with Sark and wanting to move in. Divorce is illegal here, and the law of primogeniture still applies, both designed to prevent the break-up of those original 40 tenancies. Who would want a Chief Pleas with *eighty* tenants?

11: HERM and JETHOU

And the smaller isles

BEFORE 1969 HERM WAS WELL-KNOWN to stamp-collectors as the smallest place in the world (measured by resident population) to issue its own postage stamps. The tenant – 'leaseholder' is a better description – Major Peter Wood, who was charged with administering the island when he took over its lease from the States of Guernsey in 1949, reintroduced the Herm postal service, which sold the stamps which carried the mails from Herm to Guernsey, but letters also had to have British stamps for the rest of their journey.

Herm's commemorative issue marking the Queen's visit to the island in 1957 was highly popular, as were the penny stamps cut diagonally in half and used as half-penny stamps when the real ha'penny ones were out of print. But in 1969 Britain's General Post Office became a corporation and the Channel Islands, with the Isle of Man, opted for their own postal services. From a peak of 200,000 postings a year, the Herm Post Office went to zero.

Shell Beach. The States of Guernsey bought Herm from the Crown in 1946 for £15,000, Major Wood, the second 'tenant,' having to complete near-total restoration of the island's buildings after the German occupation. He opened it up for tourism for the first time; earlier tenants, such as Sir Compton Mackenzie who leased Herm from the Crown, had allowed visitors to land and visit Shell Beach, but had banned them from everywhere else. Major Wood's policy was to realise the island's entire potential, beginning with Shell Beach on the north-east shore, where low tide reveals many thousands, perhaps millions, of sea shells in 200 species (some say 500), ranging from spirals as small as a match-head, to limpets 2in (5cm) across, and including several not known elsewhere in these latitudes; one theory among many claims that the Gulf Stream carries them from Mexico.

The island's other main attraction is its peace and solitude. Even though several hundred people may come by boat on peak days, Herm is large enough to swallow them, yet small enough to allow them to walk around its 4.5 miles (7.2km) of coastline at leisure. The isle stretches 1.5 miles (2.5km) north to south, by 0.6 mile (3,000ft, 1km) east to west; it's rocky and wooded in the south, with some imposing cliffs, while the northern third is grass-covered sand dunes home to hundreds of rabbits; this is probably what prompted the Roman name of *Erimus,* 'open and fruitless.'

White House. The community is small, with a resident population seldom more than 60, excluding summer helpers. The main buildings are the 92-bed White House Hotel overlooking the harbour, and **Le Manoir,** the Manor House, around 150ft (45m) above sea level at the centre of the island: the highest point, 203ft (62m) is a little to the south. The Manor is a castle-like building whose previous occupants have included **Prince Blücher von Wahlstatt,** great-grandson of the man who helped Wellington defeat Napoleon at Waterloo; **Sir Compton Mackenzie** who lived here 1920-'23, but set his best-seller *Whisky Galore,* published 1947, on the Hebridean isle of Eriskay; and **Sir Percival Perry,** chairman of Ford Motors who took over in 1923 and issued Herm's first postage stamps in 1925; he stayed until 1939. Blücher added the crenellations to the manor and introduced wallabies and deer to the island, but was himself interned in 1914 as he was a German national.

St Tugual's Chapel. The L-shaped Chapel of St Tugual, near the Manor, is a small building on the site of the 6th-cent chapel that St Tugual built. Nobody knows who Tugual was, but there is reason to believe she was a Welsh companion for St Magliore who settled on Sark. The original chapel was here in 1186, according to a Bull of Pope Urban III, and later a hermit probably lived in it – but the island didn't get its name from him.

Fort Houmet and Vazon Bay are a splendid backdrop to this informal campsite.

Other buildings are the Mermaid Tavern, the Ship public house, two shops, several cottages in 'the village,' the isolated Rosière Cottage, Belvoir Cottage, and Fisherman's Cottage, now self-catering apartments – and the island prison, a domed cell by the White House and among the world's smallest jails. Herm even manages a junior school, with the teacher coming out daily from St Peter Port, but from the age of 10 all children have to be educated in Guernsey. Another unusual feature is the Round Tower on Spine Road, its steps protruding from the outside wall.

There's no resident policeman, preacher, or doctor, but two of Maj. Wood's staff are honorary constables as well as fire-fighters.

Graves. Neolithic Man came here to bury his dead – thousands of them. We still don't know who they were, and why they were brought here, but some authorities believe Herm was a graveyard for late Stone Age aristocracy from the other islands and even from France. Many of the gravestones disappeared in the 19th cent when quarrying was all the rage, but enough remain on the twin hillocks of **Le Petit Monceau** and **Le Grand Monceau,** on the sandy flats. To the north was **La Pierre aux Rats,** 'the Misers' Stone,' an ancient monolith which had been a seamark for centuries until the quarrymen destroyed it. There was such an outcry of protest that they had to replace it with the stone you see today.

Quarries. It was in the 19th cent that Herm granite became popular, and quarries scarred the landscape at La Rosière; Le monceau, north of the harbour; and on the dunes. By 1830 around 400 people lived on the island, hewing and dressing the rock, and after they built Herm's own harbour, they shipped stone to Guernsey and later to Britain, where some of it was used in the new steps to St Paul's Cathedral. Locally, the rock built the Manor, the little jail, the White House, probably Bréhou Tower on an islet between Herm and Guernsey, and finally St Peter Port's harbour walls, after which demand faded and the quarries closed. The old crane at the harbour is a lone survivor of the trade.

Day visitors to Herm will almost always use both the landing points, the harbour itself at high tide, and the Rosière Steps to the south at low water.

Birds. Herm is a minor paradise for birds, with a survey in the 1980s revealing 92 species, most of them seabirds. As visitors are requested not to pick the many varieties of wild flowers, Herm has managed to become a popular tourist attraction as well as a haven of peace and quiet – probably because there are so few motor vehicles on the island.

Accommodation. Your choice from the White House Hotel, self-catering apartments, or camping on Little Seagull field – bring your tent or hire one.

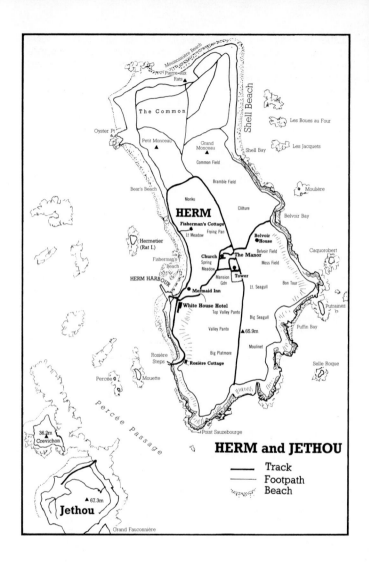

HERM and JETHOU

— Track
— Footpath
⋯⋯⋯ Beach

JETHOU

Sir Compton Mackenzie moved to Jethou – pronounced *zhuh-too* – when he left Herm in 1923, but you'll not see inside his granite house as the tenant, lawyer A G Duckworth, who bought the lease in 1984 for more than £500,000, does not encourage visitors, although Guernsey residents have the right to collect *vraic* (seaweed) and catch sandeels. Mr Duckworth's main home is in the Cayman Islands.

Pirate and smuggler. The 18th-cent house was probably the work of **John Allaire,** a privateer – a legally-approved pirate – who may also have planted the mulberry tree claimed to be the oldest in the British Isles. Allaire, who used Jethou as a warehouse for contraband and lent money to the Seigneur of Sark, probably attacked British ships as well as French, and he had a reputation for letting his victims drown rather than take prisoners. Legend claims that after his death in 1852, his gold was taken to the bank in a wheelbarrow. A later inhabitant was Lt-Col Fielden whose lease was terminated in 1867 when he was caught using the island as a warehouse for smuggled brandy; times changed so rapidly.

Recent tenants have included Angus and Susan Faed of Jersey (1964-'71, £25,000), and industrialist Sir Charles Hayward (1971-'83, £90,000) who closed the island to visitors. Lord Perry wanted to buy the lease so he could grow poisonous plants for the chemical industry, but Sir Compton refused to sell.

The tenant, whoever he may be, is exempt from Income Tax, merely paying a small annual ground rent.

Herm's charms are evident before you step ashore.

Restauld. The first known resident of 45-acre (18ha) Jethou was Restauld or Restald, 11th-cent master mariner for Duke Robert of Normandy. Restauld later became a monk and received the island as a gift from Duke Robert; it passed to the Abbey of Mont St Michel and in 1416 to the Crown of England when Henry V closed all foreign religious houses. The Crown still owns it.

Quarrying. The quarrying craze which hit Herm, spilled over to Jethou and to its satellite isle of **Crevichon,** accessible on foot from Jethou at low tide.

THE SMALLER ISLANDS

Les Casquets. The Casquets reef 5 miles (8km) west of Alderney has wrecked many ships, including the *Blanch Nef* in 1120, in which Henry I's only legitimate son, William, drowned. The first lighthouse, built in 1726, had a coal fire; later lights were St Peter, St Thomas and Donjon, on the highest rock which reaches 100ft (30m) above sea level.

Les Ecréhous. North-east of Jersey and almost half way to Carteret lie Les Ecréhous, a few tiny islands on a dangerous reef; on a clear day at low tide they're just visible from Jersey. In 1961 Jerseyman Alphonse le Gastelois took up permanent residence in the islands where he stayed for 14 years, but Phillipe Pinel, also from Jersey, lived on the islands from 1848 to 1892 and became known as the 'King of the Ecréhous.' The reef has long been accepted as part of St Martin's parish, Jersey, but the French challenged tradition at the International Court of Justice at The Hague in 1953 and claimed the reef. The court decided it was British territory.

Les Minquiers. Due south of Jersey and half way to St Malo lies the 'Minquies' reef, also decreed to be British territory at The Hague in 1953 after the French claimed it to be a dependency of the Chausey Islands. Both reefs have permanent houses on them.

Les Iles Chausey. Midway between the Minkies and Granville, the Chausey Isles were returned to French rule at the Peace of Aix-la-Chapelle in 1668. The main land is Grande Ile, holding the tiny village of Blainvillais, a fort of 1866 and another built in 1928 for Louis Renault the car manufacturer. There are also a church, lighthouse, school, shop, and several hotels, reached by small boat from Granville; around 50 islets remain at high tide, with vast reefs exposed at low water.

The Chausey Isles issued their own postage stamps in 1961 until the French Government suppressed them in 1963, six years after Herm's postal service was withdrawn. Living on a tiny island certainly creates an air of independence – could the larger islands be a little bit envious?

12: WHEN THE SUN GOES DOWN

Where to stay in the Bailiwick

THIS LIST OF ACCOMMODATION in Guernsey and its smaller islands is taken from information supplied by the Guernsey Tourist Board, PO Box 23, White Rock, St Peter Port, ✆0481.723552, fax ~714951, which can supply more information and arrange a booking at no extra cost. Or contact your tour operator.

The Guernsey Tourist Law, which also applies to Herm, states that all accommodation rented to two or more persons, must be inspected and licensed; it is graded by crowns, not stars.

The symbols ⇔ indicate the number of bedspaces; ♈ shows if there is a full liquor licence (residents can be served at any time); and ⇗ marks the presence of a pool on the premises – usually open-air.

Prices Prices are not controlled, the island's most expensive being the Royal on Glategny Esplanade, St Peter Port, rising to around £230 per person per day, full board, the next being the St Pierre Park at Rohais at less than half. The cheapest are several one-crown hotels asking little more than £10 per person for bed-and-breakfast.

Addresses. Letters in the address indicate the parish:

A	St Andrew	**M**	St Martin
C	Câtel	**Sm**	St Sampson
F	Fôret	**Sv**	St Saviour
PP	St Peter Port	**T**	Torteval
PW	St Peter-in-the-Wood	**V**	Vale

5-CROWN HOTELS
Duke of Richmond, Cambridge Park, PP, ⇔146 ♈ ⇗; **La Grande Mare,** Vazon Bay, C, ⇔125 ♈ ⇗; **Old Government House,** Ann's Place, PP, ⇔168 ♈ ⇗; **St Pierre Park,** Rohais, PP, ⇔274 ♈ ⇗.

4-CROWN HOTELS
Atlantique, L' Perelle Bay, Sm, ⇔61 ♈ ⇗; **Bella Luce,** La Fosse, M, ⇔70 ♈ ⇗; **Cobo Bay,** Cobo, C, ⇔79 ♈; **Collinette, La,** St Jacques, PP, ⇔49 ♈ ⇗; **Dolphin,** Rohais, PP, ⇔29 ♈; **Fregate, La,** Les Cotils, PP ⇔22; **Friquet, Le,** Rue du Friquet, C, ⇔48 ♈ ⇗; **Green Acres,** Les Hubits, M, ⇔99 ♈ ⇗; **Havelet, de** Havelet, PP ⇔66 ♈ ⇗; **Hougue du Pommier,** Rte de la Hougue du Pommier, C, ⇔95 ♈ ⇗; **Hougue**

Fouque Farm, La, Rue des Bas Courtils, Sv, ☎39 ♉ ⚘; Idlerocks, Jerbourg Point, M, ☎57 ♉ ⚘; Moore's, Pollet, PP, ☎93 ♉; Peninsula, Les Dicqs, V, ☎322 ♉ ⚘; Royal, Glategny Esplanade, PP, ☎58 ♉ ⚘; St Margaret's Lodge, Forest Rd, M, ☎99 ♉ ⚘; Trelade, La, Forest Rd, M, ☎96 ⚘.

3-CROWN HOTELS

Abbey Court, Les Gravées, PP, ☎60; Ambassador, Sausmarez Rd, M, ☎42; Ancresse Lodge, L' L'Ancresse Bay, V, ☎54 ♉; Barbarie, La, Saints Bay Rd, M, ☎49 ♉; Bedford, Queens Rd, PP, ☎44; Bon Port, Moulin Huet, M, ☎38 ♉ ⚘; Braye Lodge, Ruette Braye, PP, ☎47 ♉ ⚘; Chalet, Le, Fermain Bay, M, ☎93 ♉; Chêne, Le, Forest Rd, F, ☎53 ⚘; Cloche, La, Les Traudes, M, ☎22 ⚘; Douvres, Les, La Fosse, M, ☎42 ♉ ⚘; Duke of Normandy, The, Le Febvre St, PP, ☎88 ♉; Embruns House, Les, Rte de la Margion, C, ☎35 ♉; Favorita, La, Fermain Bay, M, ☎74 ♉; Fermain, The, Fort Rd, M, ☎90 ♉ ⚘; Fleur du Jardin, Kings Mills, C, ☎48 ♉ ⚘; Grand Lodge, ☎68 ♉ ⚘; Harton Lodge, Rue de Galaad, C, ☎52 ♉; Havelet Court, Havelet, PP, ☎24; Imperial, Pleinmont, T, ☎40 ♉; Lynton Park, Hacse Lane, V, ☎32; Mallard, The, La Villiaze, F, ☎99 ♉ ⚘; Michelle, La, Les Hubits des Bas, M, ☎93 ♉; Midhurst House, Candie Rd, PP, ☎17; Ozouets Lodge, Les, Ozouets Rd, PP, ☎32; Pandora, 52 Hauteville, PP, ☎117; Pembroke, L'Ancresse, V, ☎31 ♉; Piette, La, St George's Esplanade, PP, ☎31 ♉; Rocquettes, Les, Les Gravées, PP, ☎68 ♉; Saint Martin's Country, Les Merriennes, M, ☎142 ♉ ⚘; Saints Bay, Icart, M, ☎62 ⚘; San Marco, Havilland St, PP, ☎41 ♉; Sunnycroft, 5 Constitution Steps, PP, ☎27; Villette, La, La Villette, M, ☎94 ♉ ⚘; Wellesley, Sausmarez Rd, M, ☎22; White House, Herm, ☎92 ♉ ⚘; Windmill, Rue Poudreuse, M, ☎37 ⚘.

2-CROWN HOTELS

Albany, Queen's Rd, PP, ☎114 ♉ ⚘; Auberge du Val, Sous L'Eglise, Sv, ☎25; Belvoir Farm, Rue de la Hougue, C, ☎35 ⚘; Blue Horizon, Mont Durand, M, ☎52 ⚘; Captain Cook, Hauteville, PP, ☎49; Captain's, The, La Fosse, M, ☎19 ♉; Carrefour, The Grange, PP, ☎25 ⚘; Changi Lodge, Les Baissières, PP, ☎35 ⚘; Cordeliers, Les, Les Gravées, PP, ☎34 ♉; Dunchoille, Guelles Rd, PP, ☎46 ⚘; Ellingham, Camps du Moulin, M, ☎68 ♉ ⚘; Farnborough, Les Damouettes La, PP, ☎28; Fontainebleau, Les Crôutes, PP, ☎65 ♉ ⚘; Galaad, Le, Rue des Français, C, ☎27; Greenwood Trees, Sausmarez Rd, M, ☎34; Hamada, 89 Victoria Rd, PP, ☎16; Horizon Bleu, L' Grande Havre, V, ☎41; Lilyvale, Hougue du Pommier, C, ☎34 ⚘; Marine, Well Rd, PP, ☎28; Marton, The, Les Vardes, PP, ☎70; Queens, Grande Rue, M, ☎33 ♉; Quinta, La, Rue Maze, M, ☎34 ♉; Retraite, La, Rue des Frères, PP, ☎27; Somerset, Queen's Rd, PP, ☎74; St Georges, 21 St George's Esplanade, PP, ☎42; Sunnydene, Rue des Marettes, M, ☎46 ⚘; Treetops, Les Hubits, M, ☎43; Vazon Bay, Les Dunes, C, ☎50 ♉ ⚘; Wayside Cheer, Grandes Rocques, C, ☎83 ♉ ⚘; Wyndhams, Glategny Esplanade, PP, ☎53 ♉; Yacht Inn, South Esplanade, PP, ☎26 ♉.

1-CROWN HOTELS

Abreuveurs, Les, Les Abreuveurs, Sm, ☎31 ⚘; Ann-Dawn, Route des Capelles, Sm, ☎25; Antigua, Grand Maison Rd, Sm, ☎24; Baron Court, 11 Saumarez St, PP, ☎32; Burleigh, Brock Rd, PP, ☎26; Gareloch, Les Caches, M, ☎27; Hampshire Lodge, Rue Mainguy, V, ☎32 ♉ ⚘; Mapleton, Jerbourg Rd, M, ☎27; Sardrette, Les Canichers, PP, ☎30; Springhurst, Vale Rd, Sm, ☎22 ⚘; Triton, Les Hubits, M, ☎30; Valnord, Mount Durant, PP, ☎31.

HOTELS IN SARK

The Chief Pleas does not operate a hotel grading system, so this list is alphabetic. The GTO makes reservations.

Aval du Creux, Harbour Hill, ⇌31 ↲; **Dixcart,** Baker's Vale, ⇌47 ℞; **Moinerie, La,** near Seigneurie, ⇌23; **Petit Champ,** west Sark, ⇌33 ↲; **Sablonnerie, La,** Little Sark, ⇌39; **Stocks,** Baker's Vale, ⇌46 ↲.

HOTELS IN ALDERNEY

The Guernsey Tourist Office does not operate in Alderney, and there is no accommodation service; contact the Alderney Tourist Office at Victoria St, St Anne, ✆0481.822994, for a list of accommodation, but make your booking direct. All hotels take package tourists but, due to the water shortage on the island, don't expect swim-pools. Premises are not graded.

Belle Vue, Butes Rd, ✆822844 ⇌43 ℞; **Belle Vue Too,** Butes Rd, ✆822844 ⇌17 ℞; **Chez André,** Victoria St, ✆822777 ⇌28 ℞; **Devereux House,** Longy, ✆822549 ⇌21 ℞; **Harbour Lights,** Newtown, ✆822168 ⇌17 ℞; **Inchalla,** The Val, ✆823220 ⇌24 ℞; **Rose and Crown,** Le Huret, ✆823414 ⇌12 ℞; **Sea View,** Braye St, ✆822738 ⇌37 ℞; **Victoria, The,** Victoria St, ✆822754 ⇌17.

OTHER PLACES TO STAY

Guernsey has around 70 **guest houses** in four grades, most offering just bed-and-breakfast terms; Sark has three – the Beauvoir, Hivernage and Quatre Vents – and Herm has one, the White House.

Guernsey has around 160 **self-catering** flats, bungalows, cottages or chalets, invariably on weekly lettings, and Herm and Sark each has one; details from the GTO.

As there is no accommodation service in Alderney, independent travellers must make their own reservations. Here are the island's **guest houses:**

Aurigny Maison, Longy Rd, ✆822041, ⇌5; **Bibette,** Newtown Rd, ✆822536, ⇌6; **Braye,** Braye St, ✆823256, ⇌20; **Chanson de la Mer,** Braye Rd, ✆823137, ⇌2; **Essex Lodge,** Longy Bay, ✆823557, ⇌8; **Farm Court,** Mouriaux, ✆822075, ⇌17; **Haras, L'** Newtown Rd, 82374, ⇌10; **Maison Amicale,** Longis Rd, ✆822545, ⇌8; **Quest, Les,** Blaye, 822809, ⇌5; **St Anne's Guest House,** ✆823145, ⇌9; **St Ouen,** Longy Rd, ✆823129, ⇌2; **Saye Farm,** ✆822196, ⇌7; **Simerock,** Venelles, ✆823645, ⇌17.

CAMPING

Guernsey's camping sites are at **Fauxquets Valley Farm,** Câtel; **La Baillotere,** Vale; and **Vaugrat,** St Sampson. **Herm's** campsite is in Little Seagull Field, ✆722377 for reservations. For permission to camp on **Alderney,** ✆822914 and speak to the warden. Sark has no camp-sites.

GUERNSEY

air links 15
Allaire, John 105
Ancresse Common, L' 80-81
Aquarium 57
area 7
Aurigny Air Services 15
Bailiff (title) 20
Bailiff's Cross 49
banks 16
Battle of Flowers 79
bays: Bette, La 64
– Fermain 62
– Forge, de la 71
– Jaonnet, Le 64
– Marble 63
– Moulin Huet 63-64
– Moye, La 70
– Petit Bôt 64
– Petit Port 63
– Portelet 64
– Saints' 64
– Soldiers' 57
– Telegraph 63
– Vazon 77
Beaucette Marina 80
Bishop of Coutances 37,38
Burhou 92
buses 12
Butterfly Centre 78
buying property 27-28
calendar of events 18
caravans 10
car hire agencies 19-11
Casquets Reef 33,106
Castle Cornet 35-40,**54-56**
Câtel parish 76-79
Catioroc, Le 30,31,50
caves 70,95,98,99
Chapel of St Apolline 74
– – St George 77
Charles I 40
– II 40
Château de Marais 82
chevauchage 49
churches: Câtel 76
– Fôret 70
– St Andrew 69
– St Martin 64
– St Peter-in-the-Wood 72
– St Peter Port 57
– St Sampson 81
– St Saviour 75
– Torteval 72
– Vale 80
Civil War, English 39
Clameur de Haro 24-25,32,33
Coach House Galleries 72
concentration camps 47
Connétable (title) 21
Copper Craft 73

cost of living 16
Creux Mahie, La 70
cycle hire 11
de Carteret family 24,39,40
de la Rue, Thomas 62
disabled visitors 15
dolmens, graves, etc:
– Creux des Faies 30
– Creux ès Faies 30
– Folie, La 49
– Fouillages, Les 81
– Hougue de Déhus 29
– Longue Pierre, La 74
– Longue Rocque, La 50
– Rocque qui Sonne, La 51
– Table des Pions, La 49
– Trépied, Le 30
– Varde, La 29,81
Doyle Column 63
dress 17
Duchy of Normandy 22
Ecréhous, Les 106
Edward III 35-36
electricity 17
ferries 13-14
feudalism 19,24
flag 17
Forest parish 70
Fort Doyle 80
– Grey 72
– Hommet 77
– Pézèries 71
Friquet Flower Centre, Le 78
Gardien du Tombeau 29-30
German Occupation 43-48,56,65-68
Gold- & Silversmiths 76
Gouffre, Le 70
government 19-21
Grand'mère du Chimquière 29
graves, see dolmens
Guernsey Botanical Gardens 69
– Candles 82
– Clockmakers 69
– Herb Garden 75
– Toys 60
– Woodcarvers 76
Hanois, Les 71
Havre de Bon Repos 70
Henry I 33
Henry II 34
Henry VIII 38,41
highest point 64
Hommet Paradis I. 80
housing 27-28
Hugo, Victor 58
Icart Point 64
Iles Chausey 106
Ivy Castle 82
Jerbourg 35
Jethou 105-106
Joan of Arc 37

John, King of England 35
Koi Farm 80
legends 49-51
licensing hours 17
Lieutenant-Governor (title) 19
Lihou 73-74
Little Chapel 68
Margaret of Anjou 37
martello towers 41
Minquiers, Les 106
money 16
mopeds 11-12
motoring 9-11
Moulin Huet Pottery 65
museums: 201 Squadron 55
– Castle Cornet Maritime 55
– Folk . . . . 78–&9
– Fort Grey Maritime 50,72
– Guernsey 61
– Main Guard 55
– Occupation 45,70
– Royal Guernsey Militia 55
– Telephone 78
– Tomato 77-78
– Vallette Military 57
Napoleon 41
Niaux Mill, Les 78
Norman Conquest 32
Oatlands Craft Centre 82
Organization Todt 47,65
ormers 69
patois 25-27
Peastacks 63
petrol 10
Planel Dolls, La 72
primogeniture 59
prison 55
Privy Council 21,23
public holidays 18
railways 56
reservoir 75
Restauld 106
Romans 31
Rose Centre 69
Royal Courts 19-20,23
St Andrew parish 65-69
St Magliore 31-32
St Martin parish 62-65
St Peter-in-the-Wood parish 72-74
St Peter Port & parish 54-62
– 26 Cornet St 58
– Beau Séjour 62
– Candie Gardens 60-61
– Castle Carey 61
– Concert Hall 60
– Constitution Steps 60
– Guille-Allès Library 59
– Harbour 54
– Hauteville House 58
– oldest pillar box 60
– Old Guernsey Market 59

– Priaulx Library 61
– Royal Court House 60
– Town Gates 59
– Victoria Tower 54
St Sampson parish 81-82
– – Harbour 82
St Saviour parish 74-76
– – 's Tunnel 75
Saumarez family 60
– Park 78-79
Sausmarez family 64-65
– Manor 64
shopping hours 18
speed limits 9
States of Guernsey 20-21
Steckoll, Solomon 47
Strawberry Farm 75-76
Stroobant, Frank 45
Super Fred 62
Talbot Valley 78
telephones 17
tides 14-15
tomatoes 7,41
Torteval parish 70-72
tourist offices 18
Treaty of Caen 33
– – Calais 36,37
Tropical Gardens 75
Underground Hospital 65-68
Vale Castle 31,80
Vale parish 80-81
Vibert, Denis 47
Victoria, Queen 41
Vikings 32
Wars of the Roses 37
William the Conqueror 32,33
witchcraft 29,50
zoo 69

ALDERNEY: 83-92
air links 15
Alderney Pottery 89
Blaye 37
breakwater 42,87
Burhou 92
buses 12
car hire 11
Casquets reef 33
Church rule 37
concentration camps 47-48,88
cycle hire 11
Essex Castle 84,87
ferries 14
flag 7
fortification 38,41
forts 85-87
Garden Rocks 92
German Occupation 43
government 22
Harbour 91
Longis Common 84,88
Mannez lighthouse 91

Mesurier family, le	85,90
Milk-a-Punch Sunday	18
moped hire	12
Mouriaux House, Les	85
Museum	85,89
Nunnery, The	31,84
property	28
Race, The	89
railway	13,42,91
St Anne	89,91
– church	85,90
– Court House	90
– States Office	90
Status Insulae	84
Swinge, The	89
Telegraph Tower	83
tourist office	18,89
Vallée des 3 Vaux	91
SARK:	93-100
Allaire, John	98,105
Avenue	95
Brechou	99
caves, Boutiques, Les	98
– Dog	95
– Gouliot	99
– Victor Hugo	99
Chief Pleas	22-23,95
colonised	38-39
Coupée, La	100
Creux Harbour	93
Dixcart Bay	95
Eperquerie Common, L'	93
ferries	14
feudalism	24-25

flag	17
German Occupation	43
government	22-23
Grève de la Ville	95
Harbour Hill	94
horse carriages	13,94
lighthouse	94
Little Sark	100
Maseline Harbour	93
Pilcher Monument	99
pools	100
prison	23,99
property	28
rowing race	18
St Peter's Church	95
Sark Lark	99-100
Seignurie	95-96
silver mines	41,96-98,100
tourist office	18
windmill	99
Window	98
HERM:	101-104
Blücher, Prince	102
Grand Monceau	103
Mackenzie, Sir Compton	101-102,105
Manoir, Le	102
Perry, Sir Percival	102
Petit Monceau	103
postal service	101-102
prison	103
quarries	103
St Tugual's Chapel	102
Shell Beach	101
White House	102

The Chief Pleas of Sark is by day one of the island's schools.